I0829014

CHRIS GREER
PRESS

CAREER STRATEGY UNDER BROKEN LEADERSHIP

Career Strategy Under

BROKEN LEADERSHIP

THE PROFESSIONAL OPERATING SYSTEM

CHRIS GREER

CHRIS GREER PRESS

Published by Chris Greer
Printed in the United States of America

Cover Art by Chris Greer

First Edition

ISBN: 978-1-972194-04-1

CONTENTS

INTRODUCTION

The Operator's Premise

You are good at your job. Not from vanity, but from evidence. You deliver results. You solve problems others cannot or will not solve. You have built expertise, earned respect from your colleagues, and have developed the professional judgment that comes from years of sustained, competent work.

And the person above you — the person whose assessment determines your trajectory, whose advocacy opens doors or fails to, whose competence shapes your daily professional experience — is not good at theirs.

Perhaps they avoid every conversation that might produce tension, leaving your team to navigate unresolved conflicts without leadership. Perhaps they were placed in the role through relationships rather than capability, and the gap between their authority and their understanding creates problems you spend your weeks quietly solving. Perhaps they absorb credit for work they did not do, or micromanage work they do not understand, or simply occupy a leadership position without performing its functions.

You have tried what professionals try. Clear communication. Benefit of the doubt. Working harder, hoping that performance alone would produce the trajectory your capability warrants.

It has not. And you are beginning to recognize that it will not. Organizational systems do not self-correct on any timeline useful to your career, and waiting for correction primarily benefits the people whose dysfunction you are absorbing.

You are correct.

The Thesis

Leadership quality is an environmental variable. Career trajectory is not.

Organizations do not reliably select for leadership competence. Internal promotion rewards visibility and tenure as often as capability. External hiring evaluates interview performance rather than actual leadership behavior. Correction mechanisms (performance reviews, 360-degree feedback, HR intervention) rarely operate with the speed or precision the problem demands.

This is structural. The systems designed to identify, develop, and retain effective leaders fail in predictable ways, producing a steady output of leaders who cannot do what the role demands.

Every professional will spend significant portions of their career reporting to one of them.

This book will not fix that reality. It teaches you to operate within it, with the clarity that comes from understanding the system you are in rather than resenting the system you expected. The infrastructure built in that process outlasts the dysfunction that demanded it — what begins as navigation becomes the permanent operating system of a self-directed career.

The Strategic Operator

The **Strategic Operator** is a professional who treats their career as an engineered system rather than a series of reactions to organizational circumstance.

It is not a personality type. It is an orientation: diagnostic precision combined with strategic composure, organizational awareness combined with personal integrity, career ambition disciplined by the patience to play the long game.

Strategic Operators see organizations clearly: how power operates, how decisions are made, how reputations are built and destroyed, how trajectories are shaped by forces beyond individual performance.

Strategic Operators act within the system as it exists. The professional who refuses to engage with organizational reality on its own terms is not principled. They are strategically disadvantaged.

Strategic Operators build infrastructure independent of any single relationship — credibility through multiple channels, influence through strategic communication, documentation that protects their position, and the optionality to move when the calculus demands it. Their trajectory is engineered, not hoped for.

This orientation is developed. The professional who enters this book frustrated and reactive will leave it with a different relationship to the challenges they face. Not because the challenges will have changed. Because they will have.

The Reader

This book is for the professional in the middle. Not entry-level. Not executive.

The mid-career professional: operations manager, project lead, senior individual contributor, technical specialist, program manager. Someone who has built real expertise and discovered that expertise alone does not produce the trajectory it warrants. The professional with five to fifteen years of experience. Often more competent than the person evaluating their competence. Frustrated, but not yet cynical. Looking for a framework, not a complaint.

The professional ready to stop asking *Why is my leader so bad?* and start asking *What system am I in, and how do I operate within it?*

A necessary boundary: this book addresses organizational dysfunction that is legal, common, damaging to careers, and structurally persistent. It is not a guide for harassment, discrimination, or illegal workplace behavior. Those situations require legal counsel and protections these frameworks cannot replace.

A note on scope: these strategies assume organizations with layered hierarchies, the structural complexity that creates skip-level relationships, cross-functional dynamics, and political landscapes to navigate. They also assume access to organizational channels, and access is not equally distributed. Race, gender, age, and organizational culture shape whose strategic visibility is received as leadership and whose is received as presumption. The diagnostic framework assumes the reader's assessment is substantially accurate. It is designed to sharpen diagnosis, not reinforce grievance, and the possibility that your reading is incomplete is worth holding alongside the tools that help you act on what you do see.

A necessary distinction: this is not a venting manual, not anti-management rhetoric. Leadership selection systems are imperfect, not corrupt, and many leaders are excellent. The Strategic Operator does not endure dysfunction. They build capability, credibility, and trajectory through it.

The Strategic Operator Framework

The book teaches a five-phase operating system: a cycle that applies to every organizational context a professional encounters across a career.

DIAGNOSE → STABILIZE → INFLUENCE → POSITION → EVOLVE

Diagnose the System. Part I dismantles the assumption that organizations select for leadership competence and provides a diagnostic framework for the specific patterns of dysfunction you are navigating. Diagnosis replaces frustration with clarity.

Stabilize Your Foundation. Part II addresses emotional regulation, credibility-building, and professional sustainability: the internal infrastructure that enables strategic operation rather than reactive survival.

Build Strategic Influence. Part III provides the operational tools for affecting outcomes from below: adaptive communication, documentation, and the calibrated use of escalation.

Engineer Your Trajectory. Part IV widens from the direct reporting relationship to the organizational landscape: political fluency, visibility, leverage, and the strategic decisions about movement that determine long-term trajectory. The capabilities developed under broken leadership are the same capabilities that govern advancement in any organization.

Evolve Into Leadership. Part V converts adversity into curriculum: the practice of leading before formal authority arrives, the discipline of not replicating the patterns you endured, and the long view that transforms strategy into legacy.

The phases are sequential in logic, each building on its predecessors. They are simultaneous in practice, operating concurrently once established. And they are cyclical across a career: every new role, every new leader, every new organizational context activates the cycle again. Each iteration is faster and deeper.

Before You Begin

Five questions to orient yourself within the system this book describes.

Diagnostic clarity. Can you name the specific pattern of dysfunction you are navigating — not the general frustration, but the mechanism? If the answer is vague, Part I is where your work begins.

Emotional stability. When your leader makes a decision you know is wrong, what happens to your composure? If regulation is inconsistent, Part II provides the infrastructure.

Upward influence. Can you communicate with your leader in terms they can receive, not the terms you wish they could? If influence feels futile, Part III develops the capability.

Career positioning. Do you understand the political dynamics shaping your trajectory? Do you have visibility with decision-makers and options that give you strategic choice? If you feel stuck, Part IV provides the framework.

Leadership development. Are you extracting lessons from the dysfunction you observe, or merely enduring it? Are you practicing leadership regardless of title? If the adversity feels like pure cost, Part V converts it.

This book will not make your leader competent. It will not fix your organization's promotion system.

It will change your relationship to all of it: frameworks for understanding the systems you operate in, tools for navigating them strategically, and a professional identity defined by your standards rather than by the quality of the person above you.

The dysfunction is not going away. What changes is you.

A Note on the Professionals in This Book

Throughout these chapters, we follow two professionals whose experiences illustrate the Strategic Operator journey at different stages.

Elena Vasquez is a senior program manager with nine years of experience in a mid-sized technology services company. She consistently delivers complex cross-functional projects, earns respect from peers, and has been recognized in passing by senior leaders. Yet she has been passed over for promotion twice. Her direct manager, David, is well-liked but chronically avoids any situation that might create conflict including advocating for his team. Elena is learning to see her situation clearly and beginning to operate strategically within it.

Marcus Chen is a director of operations with fourteen years of experience, currently at a healthcare technology company. He leads a 40-person department and reports to James, a senior vice president who was placed in the role through executive relationships rather than operational expertise. Marcus has navigated multiple forms of leadership dysfunction across his career and has developed the composed, long-game thinking that characterizes a mature Strategic Operator. His experience demonstrates what sustained strategic practice produces.

Elena and Marcus are composites: their situations drawn from patterns observed across industries, combined and adapted to protect privacy while preserving the dynamics that matter. Their challenges are real. Their evolution is representative. Their thinking reflects the Strategic Operator mindset this book aims to develop.

When Elena appears, she is often learning — recognizing patterns, adjusting strategies, building capability. When Marcus appears, he typically demonstrates what experienced operation looks like — calibrated, patient, strategically composed. Together, they represent the arc from frustrated professional to Strategic Operator.

PART I: DIAGNOSE THE SYSTEM

Chapter 1: The Leadership Competence Illusion

The Gap Between Selection and Leadership

You have watched someone get promoted who should not have been. You knew it before they started. The people around you knew it. The organization proceeded anyway. Organizations operate on a foundational assumption: despite their flaws, hierarchies ultimately place qualified people in positions of authority. The assumption runs deep. If someone holds a leadership title, they must have demonstrated the capability to lead. The promotion was earned. The hire was vetted. The authority is legitimate.

This assumption is comforting. It suggests that the professional world operates on a rough meritocracy: imperfect but functional. Develop your skills, deliver results, demonstrate readiness, and you too will eventually rise. The system rewards competence. The hierarchy reflects capability.

The assumption is also, across most organizations, incorrect.

Not as a matter of cynicism or grievance, as a matter of structure. **The systems that place people into leadership positions — whether through internal promotion or external hiring — are not the same systems that would identify who should lead.** Understanding this disconnect is where strategy begins.

The Internal Promotion Gap

Organizations promote people. This is unremarkable. What deserves closer examination is what they promote people for.

Consider the typical path. A professional performs well in their role: they close sales, write code, manage projects, analyze data. Their performance is visible. Their results are measurable. Over time, they become the obvious candidate when a leadership position opens.

None of this demonstrates that they can lead.

Leadership requires capabilities that individual contributor success does not test: setting direction under uncertainty, developing people with different motivations, navigating organizational politics, making decisions with incomplete information, managing conflict across audiences with different needs. These are distinct skills. Some exceptional individual contributors possess them. Many do not. And nothing in the typical promotion process reliably assesses whether they do.

What the promotion process does assess, often implicitly, is visibility, likability, tenure, and the absence of obvious disqualifying behaviors. Whether the candidate can actually do what the new role requires is assumed rather than evaluated.

The result is predictable: many people are promoted into leadership based on capabilities that are necessary but not sufficient. They were excellent at what they did before. They are not excellent — and may never become excellent — at what they must do now.

The failure is not personal. They performed well and were rewarded with more responsibility. The organization's promotion criteria do not measure what the role actually requires.

The Peter Principle identified this mechanism over fifty years ago: organizations promote based on current-role performance until individuals reach position they cannot perform. A recent study of over fifty thousand employees confirmed it with uncomfortable precision: the highest-performing individual contributors, when promoted, produced the worst managerial outcomes. The attributes that earned the promotion predicted the failure. The observation endures because the structural incentive has not changed.

The External Hiring Gap

If internal promotions produce leadership failures through one set of distortions, external hiring produces them through another.

Organizations turn to external candidates believing they will avoid the limitations of internal talent pools: proven success elsewhere, fresh perspective, no political baggage. The logic seems sound. The results frequently aren't.

When hiring externally, organizations cannot directly observe a candidate's leadership capability. They observe proxies: résumé pedigree, prior titles, brand-name companies, executive presence in interviews. A VP title at a prestigious company indicates that someone achieved a VP title at a prestigious company. It does not indicate they can lead effectively in a different organization, culture, or competitive context.

The signals that impress hiring committees (polished communication, confident narratives about past successes, the halo of recognized employers) are precisely the signals interview processes are designed to detect. They are also signals that can be cultivated independent of actual leadership capability.

There is also the problem of portability. Leadership competence developed in one context does not automatically transfer to another. The executive who built a high-performing team in a fast-moving startup may stumble in a bureaucratic enterprise requiring political navigation rather than speed. The leader who thrived in a turnaround may create chaos in a stable organization needing continuity. Their prior success was real. It depended on conditions that no longer exist.

Sometimes the distortion runs deeper. Organizations hire externally not because external candidates are objectively stronger, but because they believe an outsider will solve problems that feel intractable. The hire is made partly on capability and partly on organizational hope. When the savior fails to save, the disappointment is proportional to the expectations that preceded them.

The result mirrors internal promotions: people placed into leadership based on assessments that do not predict performance in context.

Why Organizations Get This Wrong

If the misalignment between selection criteria and leadership requirements is so predictable, why do organizations persist in it?

The question assumes that organizations are designed to optimize for leadership quality. Most are not.

Organizations are designed to achieve business objectives: revenue, growth, efficiency, market position. Leadership quality matters to those objectives, but it is one variable among many, and its effects are often indirect and delayed. A sales team can hit quarterly targets under mediocre leadership. A product can succeed despite management dysfunction. Organizations can operate profitably for extended periods while leadership failures accumulate costs that won't materialize until later.

This creates a fundamental problem: the feedback loop between leadership quality and organizational outcomes is slow and noisy. Good leadership produces benefits that are difficult to isolate. Poor leadership produces costs that are dispersed, delayed, and easily misattributed.

Consider what happens when a competent professional leaves because of leadership failures. The organization records a departure. Perhaps an exit interview captures sanitized feedback. The institutional knowledge lost, the relationships that must be rebuilt, the ramp-up time for a replacement, the signal sent to remaining team members. These costs are real but invisible. They don't appear on any dashboards that executives see.

Meanwhile, the metrics that are visible (project completion, sales numbers, operational throughput) continue to be met, often because competent professionals below the dysfunctional leader compensate for their failures. The professionals absorb the cost, the organization sees the output, and the leadership failure remains hidden.

Leadership problems persist because the costs are real but not measured. The signals that would trigger correction don't surface until the damage is severe. By then, the causal chain is obscured.

The Visibility Trap

If organizations select leaders based on what they can see, the question becomes: what do they see?

What organizations see is shaped by who has access, who communicates effectively, who is present in the rooms where decisions are made, and who frames their contributions in terms that resonate with evaluators.

Two professionals contribute equally to a project's success. One presents findings to senior leadership; the other does the underlying analysis. The organization sees the presenter. The analyst's contribution exists, but it exists invisibly, filtered through someone else's narrative. When selection decisions arise, the differential in perceived contribution may have little relationship to the differential in actual contribution.

This visibility trap affects leadership selection directly. Professionals who are effective at organizational communication (presenting in meetings, managing stakeholder relationships, articulating progress in executive terms) appear more ready for leadership than those whose excellence is primarily in execution. Sometimes they are. The correlation is not reliable.

Elena Vasquez learned this early in her career, when a colleague with a smaller project portfolio but stronger executive relationships was promoted ahead of her. The decision was frustrating but not illegible. Looking back, Elena recognizes that she had assumed her work would speak for itself. It was a reasonable assumption. It was also incomplete.

"I thought the results would be obvious," Elena reflects. "What I didn't understand was that results have to be made obvious. Someone has to connect them to what leadership cares about. If you don't do that — or if someone else does it better — the results exist but they don't register."

Organizations select based on perception. Perception is shaped by visibility.

Visibility is not automatically correlated with contribution or capability. The professional who understands this can navigate it. The one who doesn't may spend years wondering why demonstrated excellence doesn't produce expected advancement.

Political Capital and Its Distortions

Beyond visibility, another factor shapes selection decisions: the accumulation and deployment of political capital.

Political capital (the relationships, alliances, and accumulated goodwill that enable professionals to influence decisions) is built through reciprocity, loyalty, collaboration, and strategic positioning. It is not inherently corrupt.

The distortion arises when political capital becomes the primary determinant of leadership selection, overriding capability. This happens more frequently than formal organizational narratives acknowledge.

A leader with strong relationships to executive sponsors may be insulated from accountability for performance failures. An external hire championed by a board member arrives with political capital they did not earn, creating similar insulation. A rising internal professional without such relationships may be held to a stricter standard, their failures attributed to personal shortcomings rather than contextual factors.

This dynamic perpetuates itself. Leaders who achieved their positions through political capital rather than capability are likely to reward loyalty over performance in their own teams, replicating the pattern that elevated them.

None of this makes organizations unusually corrupt. It makes them human institutions operating according to predictable social dynamics. The professional who expects selection decisions to operate purely on merit is misreading the system.

Short-Term Metrics and Long-Term Damage

Another structural factor reinforces the selection-competence gap: the temporal mismatch between how leadership is evaluated and when leadership quality manifests.

Organizations evaluate performance on quarterly and annual cycles. These timeframes are reasonable for measuring output. They are inadequate for measuring leadership quality, which manifests over much longer periods.

A leader who drives short-term results through unsustainable pressure may appear successful on quarterly metrics while building conditions for burnout, turnover, and institutional knowledge loss. A leader who invests in team development and sustainable processes may underperform on short-term metrics while creating conditions for long-term excellence. The organization's evaluation systems will likely reward the first and question the second.

This temporal mismatch creates perverse incentives. Professionals learn that visible short-term results matter more than sustainable long-term contribution.

The organization does not learn, because the feedback arrives too late to inform the decisions that produced it.

The Psychological Experience of Structural Failure

For the competent professional working under incompetent leadership, these structural dynamics often remain invisible. What is visible is the immediate experience: the frustrating decisions, the lack of direction, the missed opportunities, the organizational choices that seem to reward the wrong things.

Without a structural lens, this experience becomes personalized. The professional wonders what they are doing wrong. They question whether their perception is accurate. Perhaps the leader has capabilities they cannot see. They wonder if they are being too critical, too impatient, too demanding of standards the organization never promised to uphold.

This self-questioning is natural and sometimes accurate. But when it stems from misunderstanding organizational dynamics rather than genuine self-assessment, it becomes corrosive. The professional begins to distrust their own judgment. They lower their standards to match what the system appears to reward. They disengage from excellence that goes unrecognized. Or they escalate frustration until it damages their standing, confirming the very narrative they were trying to resist.

Recognizing that the problem is structural, not personal, changes the frame. The leader's incompetence is not random bad luck. It is a predictable outcome of systems that select for the wrong things, measure the wrong outcomes, and operate on the wrong timeframes. This recognition does not reduce the frustration. It changes the question from "why is this happening to me" to "how do I operate within it."

The Myth of Eventual Correction

A persistent assumption among professionals navigating leadership dysfunction is that the organization will eventually recognize and correct the problem. The leader will be exposed. Their failures will become undeniable. The system will self-correct.

Sometimes this happens. More often, it takes far longer than it should, if it happens at all.

The reasons are structural. Leaders who achieved their positions through political capital often retain the political capital that protects them. Their failures may be visible to direct reports but invisible, or framed differently, to the decision-makers who could intervene. The costs of their leadership are diffuse and difficult to attribute. The political costs of removing them may exceed the operational costs of retaining them.

There is also institutional investment. An organization that selected someone into leadership has implicitly endorsed that person's capability. Reversing the endorsement creates uncomfortable questions about the judgment of those who made the decision. It is often easier to transfer the leader, wait for them to leave voluntarily, or simply endure the costs than to take action that requires acknowledging a selection failure.

Do not rely on organizational correction as a strategy. It may happen. It may not. And the timeline, if it does happen, may exceed what is sustainable for your career. Operating effectively regardless of whether correction arrives is the only reliable strategy.

Recalibrating Expectations

None of this requires cynicism. Cynicism is its own dysfunction: a withdrawal from engagement based on the conclusion that nothing matters. That conclusion is incorrect.

What changes is the expectation that organizational systems will reliably recognize and reward excellence. They may. They often don't. The recognition is uneven, delayed, and filtered through dynamics that have little to do with merit.

The professional who expects merit to be recognized automatically will be repeatedly disappointed and may conclude, incorrectly, that the problem is their own inadequacy. The professional who understands that recognition requires active management, including visibility, relationships, and strategic positioning, can pursue excellence while also ensuring that excellence is perceived. Both matter. Neither is sufficient alone.

The organization is not a reliable judge of your value. It is a complex system operating according to incentives that may or may not align with your interests.

From Understanding to Operation

The leader promoted beyond their competence requires different navigation than the political appointee. The executive installed for relationships creates different challenges than the external hire who could not translate past success.

Structural recognition changes the question. Diagnostic precision changes what you do about it.

What follows: the specific archetypes of leadership failure, and what each demands from the professionals navigating them.

Chapter 2: The Six Faces of Failure

A Diagnostic Taxonomy of Leadership Dysfunction

The most common mistake professionals make when facing incompetent leadership is treating all dysfunction as the same problem.

It rarely is.

A leader who avoids conflict requires a fundamentally different navigation strategy than one who micromanages without expertise. A leader elevated beyond their capability creates different challenges than one installed for political reasons. The professional who responds to an absent authority with the same approach they'd use for a credit absorber will find the strategy failing — and the failure will appear to be theirs.

The type of leadership failure determines which strategies will work and which will backfire.

The Diagnostic Imperative

Most professionals misdiagnose their leadership situation, and that misdiagnosis has costs.

The error usually runs in one of two directions. Some professionals over-personalize, attributing dysfunction to malice or character flaws when the actual cause is structural: a leader operating beyond their competence ceiling, or constrained by pressures invisible to their team. Others under-diagnose, assuming all difficult leadership is essentially the same and responding with generic frustration rather than targeted strategy.

Both errors produce ineffective responses. The professional who believes their leader is deliberately sabotaging them adopts adversarial postures that create unnecessary conflict. The one who treats a Conflict Avoider identically to a Credit Absorber wastes energy on strategies that don't address the actual problem.

Accurate diagnosis requires separating three distinct questions. What is the observable behavior: not interpretation, not motive, but what does this leader actually do and not do? What is the likely source: a skill deficit, a will deficit, or a structural constraint? And what does this mean strategically: given this diagnosis, what approaches are likely to succeed, and which are likely to fail?

Elena Vasquez spent her first year under her manager, David, assuming he was simply bad at his job. It wasn't until she began observing more precisely that she recognized the specific pattern: David wasn't incompetent across the board.

He was specifically avoidant of any situation that might create interpersonal tension. This distinction changed her strategy entirely. She stopped expecting him to advocate for her in contentious resource discussions and started building alternative channels for that advocacy.

"Once I understood what he specifically couldn't do," Elena reflects, "I stopped being surprised when he didn't do it. That sounds small, but it changed how I operated."

Precision requires a vocabulary for what you're observing.

The Six Archetypes

Patterns of dysfunction cluster into recognizable types, each creating distinct challenges and requiring distinct responses.

The Peter Principle Promotion

This leader was excellent at their previous role. Their elevation (whether through internal promotion or external recruitment at a higher level) was earned and made sense at the time. The problem is that the skills making them successful are structurally insufficient for their current position.

The classic pattern: a brilliant engineer promoted to lead engineers, now struggling because leading requires different capabilities than engineering. A successful director recruited to be VP, now floundering because the scope, politics, and stakeholder complexity exceed anything they navigated before. In both cases, the promotion-competence gap is in action.

What makes this archetype distinct is that the leader typically knows, at some level, that they're in over their head. This awareness can manifest as defensiveness, rigidity, or retreat into tasks they're still good at while neglecting leadership responsibilities they can't perform.

Strategic implications: This leader is structurally overwhelmed, not adversarial. They are often uncomfortable and would benefit from support, though they may be too proud or too scared to ask. Approaches that feel collaborative rather than critical produce higher success rates. Framing input as helping them succeed, rather than exposing what they're missing, addresses their insecurity without triggering defensiveness.

Common mistake: Assuming their technical credibility means they should understand concerns when presented logically. The competence gap is not cognitive — it is behavioral. They understand the concern. They cannot execute the leadership response it requires.

The Political Appointee

This leader holds their position primarily because of relationships, alliances, or political capital rather than demonstrated capability. They may have been placed by a powerful sponsor or promoted as reward for loyalty rather than performance. The Political Appointee can be a longtime insider elevated through patronage or an external hire brought in to serve political rather than operational purposes.

The Political Appointee often knows their position is relationship-dependent, which makes them highly attuned to managing upward and across to their power base while neglecting the function they nominally lead. Their primary concern is maintaining relationships that sustain their position, not optimizing team performance.

Positional authority reliably intensifies self-protective behavior. The higher the stakes of maintaining a role, the more cognitive resources are directed toward threat management and political survival rather than operational effectiveness.

This dynamic shapes daily reality for Marcus Chen, who reports to exactly this archetype. His SVP, James, was placed in the role because of his relationship with the CEO, not because he understood operations. James is not malicious. He is simply focused on what matters for his survival: his relationship with executive leadership, not the operational excellence of Marcus's division.

"James isn't trying to make my job harder," Marcus observes. "He's just not thinking about my job at all. His attention is on the people who put him in that chair and can take him out of it."

Strategic implications: This leader's incentives become clear once visible. They will prioritize what protects their political position. Framing needs as serving that position (making them look good to sponsors, avoiding problems that might embarrass them upward) creates leverage. When needs conflict with their political survival, expect to lose. Building relationships with their sponsors independently ensures access doesn't depend entirely on a leader whose attention is elsewhere.

Common mistake: Expecting them to prioritize functional excellence because it's their job. Their job, as they experience it, is maintaining the relationships that gave them the role.

The Absent Authority

This leader is physically or mentally elsewhere. They may be checked out: approaching retirement, distracted by personal circumstances, or simply disengaged from a role they no longer find meaningful. They may be spread impossibly thin across too many responsibilities. Or they may be conflict-avoidant to the point of functional absence.

The Absent Authority creates a specific kind of dysfunction: a leadership vacuum. Decisions don't get made, direction isn't provided, and resources aren't allocated. Teams figure things out themselves, often without the positional authority to do so effectively.

Strategic implications: In some ways, this is the most navigable archetype. The Absent Authority often doesn't block initiative. They simply don't engage with it. This creates space for informal leadership and building capabilities that wouldn't be possible under more controlling leadership. The risk is taking on responsibility without corresponding authority or credit. Heavy documentation helps. Building lateral relationships that validate contributions when the direct leader cannot is essential. And watching for the transition matters: when this leader eventually leaves, the power vacuum will reshape, and positioning becomes relevant.

Common mistake: Filling the vacuum so completely that exhaustion follows from doing two jobs while being compensated and recognized for one. Strategic Operators distinguish between necessary gap-filling and unsustainable overextension.

The Micromanager Without Expertise

This leader combines high control needs with low domain competence, a particularly frustrating combination. They involve themselves in decisions they don't understand, demand visibility into work they can't evaluate, and often slow execution while adding no value.

The behavior usually stems from anxiety. Not understanding the work, they cannot assess it from outcomes alone. They need to see the process, control details, reassure themselves through involvement that things are going correctly, even when their involvement makes things go worse.

Strategic implications: This archetype requires active management of their anxiety, not just the work itself. Proactive communication reduces their need to seek information. Structured updates in their preferred format address control needs without requiring them to insert themselves into execution. The goal is creating the feeling of being informed and in control without granting actual operational control.

Common mistake: Resenting the management overhead and withdrawing information, which increases their anxiety and intensifies micromanagement. The instinct to create distance usually backfires with this archetype.

A senior analyst reports to a director who demands review of every client communication before sending, despite having no background in the technical subject matter. Rather than contesting this, the analyst creates a simple template showing key points and risk assessment for each communication. The review becomes a two-minute checkpoint rather than a lengthy editing session. The director feels informed; the analyst preserves time and autonomy.

The Credit Absorber

This leader systematically claims credit for their team's work while deflecting blame for failures. In meetings with senior leadership, "we" accomplishments become "I" accomplishments. Individual contributions disappear into the leader's narrative of their own success. When problems arise, accountability flows downward.

The Credit Absorber is sometimes consciously manipulative, sometimes genuinely convinced by their own narrative. Many convince themselves that their "leadership" of the work entitles them to ownership of it. Either way, the effect is the same: people doing the work become invisible while the leader accumulates recognition.

Marcus experienced this archetype earlier in his career. The lessons still inform his approach.

"My first instinct was fighting it directly — correcting the record when she claimed my team's work," Marcus recalls. "That made me look petty and political. Worse, it didn't change anything. She still got the credit. I just looked like someone who couldn't work well with leadership."

Strategic implications: Direct confrontation rarely works and often damages the challenger more than the absorber. The effective counter-strategy is building visibility through channels they don't control: cross-functional relationships, senior stakeholders encountered independently, documentation creating an evidence trail. When work is visible from multiple angles, a single narrative can't erase it.

Common mistake: Expecting organizational systems (HR, performance reviews, senior leadership) to naturally correct the imbalance. They rarely do. Professionals who wait for correction wait indefinitely.

The Conflict Avoider

This leader cannot or will not engage with situations that might produce interpersonal tension. They avoid difficult conversations, defer hard decisions, and prioritize surface harmony over necessary confrontation. Problems fester rather than get addressed. Poor performers are tolerated rather than managed. Resource conflicts are never resolved, only smoothed over temporarily.

Elena's manager, David, is this archetype. His avoidance manifests as vague feedback, reluctance to advocate for his team when it might create tension with peers, and inability to make decisions that might displease anyone.

"David wants everyone to be happy," Elena observes. "Which means no one is, because nothing actually gets resolved. He smooths things over until they erupt somewhere else."

Strategic implications: The Conflict Avoider will not fight for you, represent your interests in contentious situations, or deliver difficult feedback to peers or leadership on your behalf. Stop expecting it. Build alternative channels for advocacy. When something is needed that would require the leader to engage in conflict, find alternative paths: going direct when possible, building coalitions with peers, or framing requests in ways that don't require opposition.

On the positive side, the Conflict Avoider often grants significant autonomy within your domain, as long as conflicts don't surface that require their management. This space can be valuable if used strategically.

Common mistake: Repeatedly escalating issues expecting resolution, then becoming frustrated when resolution doesn't come. Once the pattern is diagnosed, continuing to expect different results reflects on the professional, not the leader.

Six patterns. Six different systems operating beneath the surface of what looks, from the outside, like a single problem: bad leadership.

Most professionals never reach this level of diagnostic clarity. They experience the frustration and stop there. One undifferentiated reaction to what are, in practice, very different situations. The professional who can name the pattern they're facing has already separated themselves from the majority who cannot.

Not because the label matters. Because the label changes what they do next.

Pattern Interaction

These six archetypes describe failure mechanisms — not personalities.

The distinction matters. A personality diagnosis attempts to explain who a leader is. A failure mechanism describes what a leader does — the specific operational pattern that creates cost for the people below them. The diagnostic goal is strategic calibration: identifying the dominant pattern so that your response addresses what is actually happening rather than what you assume about why.

Leaders rarely exhibit a single pattern in isolation. The Political Appointee who lacks functional understanding may also micromanage, not from expertise, but from the anxiety that accompanies operating beyond their depth. The Peter Principle Promotion whose competence gap generates insecurity may avoid the conflicts that would expose it, producing a hybrid of two failure modes. The Absent Authority who has disengaged may, in brief moments of re-engagement, absorb credit for work they did not oversee, not from calculated appropriation, but from a distorted understanding of what occurred in their absence.

These combinations are common. So is context-dependent amplification. A leader whose conflict avoidance is manageable under stable conditions may become functionally absent during organizational crisis, when the pressure to confront intensifies, the avoidance deepens. A Political Appointee whose political maneuvering is tolerable during growth may become destructive during contraction, when the gap between political positioning and operational reality narrows to a point where both cannot coexist. Stress, rapid organizational change, and the arrival of new authority above a leader can each amplify the dominant failure mechanism or surface secondary ones that were previously latent.

The Strategic Operator does not need an exhaustive psychological profile. They need the dominant operational pattern — the mechanism producing the most significant cost — and the awareness that the pattern may shift as conditions change. The taxonomy is a diagnostic instrument, not a verdict. It prioritizes usability over comprehensiveness, strategic clarity over clinical precision. The leader you are navigating is more complex than any framework can capture. The framework does not need to capture everything. It needs to capture enough to inform your next decision.

How Dysfunction Spreads

Leadership dysfunction does not remain contained within the leader. It spreads.

Teams adapt to their leadership environment. Under a Conflict Avoider, team members learn that raising problems creates discomfort, so problems go unraised. Under a Credit Absorber, individual initiative decreases because recognition won't follow. Under an Absent Authority, shadow hierarchies emerge as informal leaders fill the vacuum. Under a Micromanager, independent thinking atrophies as people wait for direction.

The phenomenon operates as a spectrum: professionals exist somewhere on a continuum from active resistance to unconscious absorption. The longer the exposure to a dysfunctional environment, the greater the risk of drift toward absorption, adopting the very patterns being criticized without recognizing it.

This is why diagnosis must include self-diagnosis. Strategic Operators periodically ask: How is this environment changing me? What behaviors have I adopted that I wouldn't have chosen? Am I resisting the dysfunction or slowly becoming part of it?

Elena noticed this drift in herself after eighteen months under David. She had stopped raising concerns in team meetings because she knew they wouldn't be addressed, lowered her expectations for what the team could accomplish, and started avoiding her own difficult conversations, unconsciously modeling David's pattern.

"I caught myself smoothing over a conflict between two of my project leads instead of addressing it," she admits. "And I realized — that's exactly what David does. That's what I've been frustrated about. I was becoming him."

That recognition marked a turning point. Diagnosis of the leader's dysfunction had to include diagnosis of its effects on her own behavior.

From Diagnosis to Strategy

Marcus Chen frames it simply: "I've worked for four different versions of bad leadership in my career. They weren't the same problem, and they didn't have the same solutions. Once I stopped treating them as one problem, I stopped being surprised when one solution didn't work."

Diagnosis without composure produces insight that cannot be acted upon.

The dysfunction is mapped. What follows is the internal stability that makes strategic action possible.

PART II: STABILIZE YOUR FOUNDATION

Chapter 3: The Professional Stance

Emotional Regulation as Strategic Capability

You are in a meeting, or reading an email, or listening to a directive that makes no operational sense. You know the decision is wrong. You can see the downstream consequences, the wasted resources, the predictable failure. And yet the person making this decision outranks you.

In that moment, something happens internally. Frustration rises. Perhaps disbelief. Perhaps the particular exhaustion that comes from watching incompetence exercise authority over competence, again.

What you do next matters more than you think.

The instinct is to believe this moment is private. That your internal reaction is invisible to others. It is not. What happens in that moment, and in the hundreds like it across a career, shapes how you are perceived, how much influence you accumulate, and what trajectory becomes available to you.

Stability is not a personality trait. It is a professional capability. And it is one of the few variables entirely within your control.

The Strategic Case for Composure

Organizations constantly evaluate professionals for advancement, influence, and trust, usually without explicit criteria or formal assessment. These evaluations happen in meetings, in hallway interactions, in how you respond to pressure, in what your face communicates when leadership makes a questionable call.

The professionals who advance are not always the most competent. They are often the ones who appear most capable of handling increased responsibility. One of the primary signals organizations use to assess this is composure under pressure.

Consider two equally competent professionals facing the same incompetent leadership decision. The first sighs audibly in the meeting. Their body language communicates disagreement. Later, they vent to colleagues. Over time, they become known as someone who "has issues" with leadership, who "doesn't handle pressure well."

The second maintains neutral composure in the meeting. They ask clarifying questions without editorial tone. Later, they document concerns through appropriate channels and continue executing. Over time, they become known as someone who "stays calm under pressure," who "is ready for more responsibility."

Both are frustrated. Both have valid concerns. Only one is building the perception capital that creates options.

Composure is not about feeling less. It is about controlling what your feelings communicate to others.

What Instability Actually Costs

The cost of visible frustration under incompetent leadership is rarely immediate. It accumulates.

Every visible reaction to leadership dysfunction becomes part of how colleagues perceive you. These perceptions aggregate, get communicated to others, and factor into decisions about projects, promotions, and opportunities, often without your knowledge. Leaders, even incompetent ones, are less likely to accept input from professionals they perceive as hostile. The more frustrated you appear, the less capacity you have to shape outcomes. Frustration reduces influence, which increases frustration.

Organizations remember emotional moments disproportionately. A single visible loss of composure can define perception for years. Once you are perceived as "frustrated" or "negative," observers interpret even neutral behavior through that lens. A direct question becomes "challenging authority."

A pragmatic concern becomes "being difficult."

Marcus Chen learned this cost early in his career, long before he became the composed operator he is today. In his first management role, he reported to a leader who routinely claimed credit for his team's work. Marcus let his frustration show: in meetings, in emails, in conversations with peers. He was right to be frustrated. The behavior was genuinely problematic. But his visible reaction cost him a promotion that went to a less qualified peer who had maintained better relationships across the organization.

"I was correct about the problem," Marcus reflects now. "But the organization didn't reward me for identifying dysfunction. It penalized me for not handling it smoothly."

Being right about leadership failure does not protect you from the consequences of reacting poorly to it.

The Difference Between Suppression and Regulation

There is a critical distinction many professionals miss.

Suppression is forcing yourself not to feel what you feel: pretending frustration doesn't exist, pushing it down. Suppression is psychologically costly and unsustainable. It leads to cynicism, disengagement, or eventual explosive release. It also leaks: suppressed emotion finds expression in body language, tone, and micro-behaviors that observers detect even when you believe you're hiding it.

Regulation is feeling what you feel while controlling how and when it is expressed. It is acknowledging frustration privately while choosing its public expression strategically. Regulation preserves psychological authenticity while managing professional perception.

The Professional Stance is about building the capacity to choose your response rather than having your response chosen for you by circumstance.

Calibrated Affect

Strategic Operators develop calibrated affect: the ability to modulate emotional expression based on context, stakes, and strategic objectives. The professional equivalent of code-switching — adjusting communication for the environment while maintaining core identity.

Calibrated affect is specific. Intensity calibration means matching the visible intensity of your reaction to what the situation strategically requires: a genuinely serious issue may warrant visible concern, while a routine leadership failure may warrant none. Timing calibration involves choosing when to express concerns or disagreements; the middle of a meeting with senior stakeholders is rarely optimal, while a private conversation or written follow-up often provides more leverage. Channel calibration is selecting the appropriate medium: some concerns are best raised verbally and privately, others benefit from documentation, still others communicate better through questions than statements.

A supply chain manager receives a directive from her VP that will create a significant bottleneck three months downstream. Her immediate reaction is frustration; she raised this exact concern in planning meetings the VP didn't attend. Rather than expressing this in the moment, she acknowledges the directive, then sends a brief email "confirming her understanding" that includes a single line noting the timeline risk. When the bottleneck materializes later, her professional response is on record.

The Particular Challenge of Sustained Dysfunction

Calibrating affect in a single frustrating moment is one skill. Maintaining professional composure over months or years of sustained leadership dysfunction is a different challenge entirely.

Elena Vasquez is learning this distinction. Nearly two years under David. Each individual interaction is manageable. The cumulative weight is harder.

"It's not any single thing," Elena observes. "It's knowing that tomorrow will be the same. Next month will be the same. That nothing I do will change how he operates."

Elena describes a moment that clarified this for her: a quarterly review where David delivered her performance assessment in language so generic it could have described anyone on the team. She sat across from him, heard the words, and felt something tighten in her chest. Not anger exactly. Something closer to the effort of not reacting, of holding professional composure while absorbing the recognition that her manager could not describe her work with any specificity at all. She thanked him for the feedback. She walked back to her desk. She sat there for a full minute before she could focus on anything else.

That is what regulation costs. Not a single dramatic moment, but the accumulated weight of small ones.

Strategic Operators manage sustained dysfunction through deliberate practice. They compartmentalize without denial, acknowledging dysfunction while building mental boundaries that prevent it from contaminating all professional experience. They allocate attention strategically, directing focus toward work that remains satisfying and within their control. They maintain realistic timeline orientation: the current situation is a chapter, not the story. And they develop private processing systems: trusted peers outside the organization, reflection practices, channels that allow emotional processing without professional cost.

None of this makes the dysfunction acceptable. It recognizes that addressing it effectively requires sustained capability, and sustained capability requires managing the psychological load.

Building Autonomous Professional Identity

There is a deeper vulnerability that incompetent leadership exploits, often without intending to: the human need for validation.

Most professionals, particularly high performers, have spent their careers in systems that provided feedback. Good grades in school. Positive performance reviews. Recognition for achievement. Over time, this creates an implicit expectation: if I perform well, the system will acknowledge it.

Incompetent leadership breaks this expectation. The Conflict Avoider cannot articulate what you've done well because they haven't paid close enough attention. The Credit Absorber acknowledges your work by claiming it as their own. The Absent Authority provides no feedback at all. The Political Appointee evaluates based on loyalty rather than performance.

When the expected validation doesn't arrive, professionals experience something more destabilizing than frustration. They begin to question their own competence. Maybe the feedback system is accurate. Maybe their self-perception was inflated.

Unreliable leadership erodes professional self-perception from the inside.

The counter to this erosion is structural: your professional identity must be anchored in your own assessment of your competence and values, not in organizational recognition.

This requires honest self-evaluation: clear-eyed awareness of actual capabilities and limitations. But the source of that evaluation shifts from external validation to internal standards. Strategic Operators develop self-defined competence criteria: clear internal metrics for what good work looks like, independent of whether leadership can perceive them. They practice evidence-based self-assessment, collecting their own data through project outcomes, problems solved, capabilities demonstrated. They anchor in values (integrity, quality, collaboration) rather than organizational approval. And they maintain external reference points: industry peers, professional networks, mentors who provide reality checks uncorrupted by local dysfunction.

Elena has begun building this framework, though she wouldn't use that language. After her second passed-over promotion, she started keeping a private record of her project outcomes, not for documentation purposes, but for herself. When David's vague feedback leaves her uncertain about her standing, she reviews her own record. The projects are there. The results are there. David's inability to articulate them doesn't make them less real.

"I realized I was letting his perception define my reality," Elena says. "He doesn't actually know what I do. Why would I let someone who doesn't know what I do determine whether I'm doing it well?"

This recalibration is necessary — and incomplete without one discipline: frustration distorts assessment in both directions. It can erode confidence in work that deserves it, and it can inflate it, providing a convenient external explanation for every setback. These diagnostic frameworks increase precision, not confirm the assumption that dysfunction always originates outside you.

The Stability-Influence Connection

Influence flows toward professionals perceived as stable, reliable, and capable of handling difficult situations without creating additional problems. Not because organizations are wise or just. Organizational actors, including incompetent leaders, make constant, often unconscious calculations about risk.

Engaging with a visibly frustrated professional carries perceived risk: escalation, conflict, collateral damage. The path of least resistance is minimizing that engagement. Engaging with a composed professional carries less risk. Even when they disagree, they do so without collateral damage. They are safe to include in important discussions, to put in front of senior leaders, to trust with sensitive situations.

Stability increases access, which expands influence and ultimately creates options.

Marcus Chen has navigated his current situation — reporting to a Political Appointee who doesn't understand his function — by becoming the most stable, reliable presence in his division. James, his leader, has learned that Marcus will not embarrass him, will not create problems that escalate upward, will not make his leadership look worse than it already does.

This has given Marcus access his peers don't have. James consults him before making commitments, because Marcus provides calm, pragmatic input rather than criticism. James includes him in senior discussions, because Marcus can be trusted to represent the division professionally.

Marcus is not James's friend. He is not complicit in James's limitations. But he has built a professional relationship that allows him to shape outcomes despite those limitations.

This composure is not effortless. Marcus recalls a moment when James committed his division to an unrealistic delivery timeline during a board presentation — a commitment made without consulting Marcus, based on a function James doesn't understand. Marcus heard it in real time. He did not react. He took a note. He addressed it privately afterward, restructuring the timeline into something achievable while letting James present the revision as his own refinement.

"That one cost me," Marcus admits. "Not because the fix was hard. Because sitting there while someone volunteers your team for failure — and choosing not to react — requires something. It's a skill. But it's not a free one."

"I can't make James competent," Marcus continues. "But I can be the safest person for him to rely on. That gives me room to operate that I wouldn't have otherwise."

Practical Calibration

The Professional Stance requires practice: repeated application of regulatory capacity until it becomes default rather than effortful choice.

Before high-stakes interactions, take sixty seconds to consciously set your intended affect. What is the outcome you want? What perception serves that outcome? What reaction would undermine it? This brief pre-commitment makes intentional regulation more likely than reactive expression.

During frustrating moments, create a physical pause (a breath, a note-taking gesture, a sip of water) that interrupts the immediate reaction and creates space for choice. The goal is not to eliminate the internal response but to prevent its automatic external expression.

After difficult interactions, process privately and completely. The frustration is real and deserves acknowledgment, just not in the meeting where it occurred. Find appropriate channels: a trusted colleague, a written reflection, a conversation with someone outside the organization.

A project lead notices that his visible irritation in Monday planning meetings has become a running joke among team members: he's the person who "always has a problem" with leadership decisions. Recognizing this reputation is costing him influence, he commits to a deliberate practice: for three months, he asks only questions in planning meetings. No statements, no reactions, just clarifying questions. The forced constraint gradually resets his reputation, and unexpectedly, his influence with leadership increases. They now perceive him as "thoughtful" rather than "negative."

What Stability Does Not Mean

Stability does not mean agreement. Strategic Operators disagree, challenge, and push back; they simply do so with calibrated affect that maximizes influence and minimizes perception cost.

Stability does not mean passivity. It is the foundation from which strategic action becomes possible. The composed professional is more capable of effective resistance, not less.

Stability does not mean inauthenticity. Calibrated affect is intentional choice about what to express, when, and how. The underlying values and assessments remain authentic; the expression is strategic.

Stability does not mean permanence. The Professional Stance is maintained as long as it serves your strategic objectives. There may be situations (ethical violations, serious misconduct, unsustainable conditions) where visible reaction is the correct choice. Strategic Operators do not confuse composure with compliance.

The Identity Shift

When Elena began consciously developing her Professional Stance, she experienced it as a technique: something she did in specific situations to manage perception. Over time, something shifted.

"It stopped being a thing I did and started being how I thought about work," she reflects. "I used to walk into meetings ready to be frustrated. Now I walk in thinking about what I want to accomplish and what serves that goal. The frustration still shows up sometimes, but it doesn't run the show anymore."

This shift — from technique to identity — is the deeper transformation. The Professional Stance is not ultimately about managing reactions to incompetent leadership. It is about becoming a professional whose stability is an asset, whose composure creates opportunity, whose presence in difficult situations is an organizational resource.

Whether your leadership deserves your frustration is irrelevant. The only operational question is whether expressing it serves your professional objectives or undermines them.

Strategic Operators build the capacity to ask that question in the moment, and act accordingly.

Composure alone does not sustain a career. The next requirement is infrastructure: systems for building credibility independent of leadership validation.

Chapter 4: Credibility as Infrastructure

Building Reputation When Your Leader Won't

You do excellent work that no one who matters ever sees.

Your contribution passes through a filter — your direct manager — who either cannot perceive its value, cannot articulate it, or cannot be bothered to communicate it upward. The work disappears into a narrative you don't control.

The instinct is to work harder. The instinct is usually wrong. The problem is not insufficient performance. The problem is insufficient infrastructure.

The Strategic Operator builds that infrastructure: systems that make credibility visible, durable, and independent of any single unreliable channel.

The Performance-Perception Gap

Performance is what you do. Perception is what others believe about what you do — constructed from incomplete information, filtered through biases, shaped by visibility and narrative. The gap is wider than most professionals assume. When researchers decompose performance ratings, the majority of variance reflects the rater's perception — not the ratee's actual performance. The filter dominates the signal.

In functional environments, they converge over time. Under dysfunctional leadership, they diverge. The Conflict Avoider cannot articulate what you've done. The Credit Absorber claims it. The Absent Authority provides no signal at all. The Political Appointee evaluates loyalty rather than output.

The resulting gap determines what opportunities arrive and which never materialize. It affects compensation, advancement, and long-term positioning.

Closing this gap is the professional's responsibility. Waiting for a dysfunctional leader to accurately represent your value is not a strategy. Building systems that create perception independent of that leader is.

The Single-Channel Vulnerability

Most professionals operate with a single primary channel for reputation: their direct manager.

In functional environments, this works. The manager observes daily work, understands context, and has access to conversations where reputation is built or eroded. They translate contribution into terms that resonate with senior leadership.

When this channel fails (when the manager cannot or will not perform this function) the professional faces a structural problem that additional performance cannot solve.

The vulnerability is architectural. A system that depends on a single node fails when that node fails. The bottleneck determines throughput regardless of how strong the rest of the system is.

Elena Vasquez operated with this single-channel architecture for years. Her work was strong. Her results were visible to her immediate team. But everything that reached beyond her team passed through David, who filtered it into vague generalities that failed to distinguish her contributions from anyone else's. In rooms where her name might have been mentioned with specificity, it was mentioned, if at all, without substance.

"I kept thinking if I just delivered more, something would break through," Elena recalls. "What I didn't understand was that the channel itself was the constraint. More signal through a broken channel doesn't produce more reception. It just produces more signal that gets lost."

The recognition shifted her approach entirely. Not "how do I perform better?" but "how do I build additional channels?"

The Credibility Compound

Professional reputation accrues incrementally, not through single moments of visibility but through repeated small signals that aggregate into a coherent professional identity.

The Credibility Compound: each interaction, each delivered commitment, each demonstration of competence deposits into a cumulative picture that sharpens with repetition. It becomes what people "know" about you, even when they can't point to specific evidence.

The compound works in both directions. Consistent positive signals create opportunities. Absence of signals — or signals filtered through narratives you don't control — builds a reputation of invisibility that constrains them.

If your primary channel is not transmitting, your compound is not building.

Strategic Operators build the channels that carry their signals.

Building Distributed Credibility

The alternative to single-channel vulnerability is distributed credibility: reputation built through multiple independent channels that don't depend on any single node.

Self-promotion broadcasts accomplishments regardless of context or audience. Distributed credibility builds systems where your work naturally becomes visible to people who should see it.

Lateral relationships form the first layer. Peers in other functions, colleagues on cross-functional projects, professionals in adjacent teams. These relationships create witnesses to your work who exist outside your manager's narrative control. When your name comes up in conversations you're not part of, lateral relationships determine whether anyone can speak to your actual contribution.

Building these relationships requires intentionality: cross-functional collaboration even when not strictly required, genuine help to peers whose projects touch yours. Every interaction deposits into the credibility compound — not transactionally, but with awareness that professional relationships have cumulative value.

Skip-level visibility forms the second layer. Senior leaders above your direct manager are often the actual decision-makers for opportunities and advancement. If your only access to them passes through your manager, your visibility depends entirely on that filter's quality.

Strategic Operators create appropriate skip-level visibility: volunteering for projects with executive exposure, presenting in forums where senior leaders are present, building relationships through organizational activities that cross hierarchical lines. The goal is not circumvention — it is ensuring your professional identity exists in the minds of decision-makers independent of any single representation.

External credibility forms the third layer. Industry relationships, professional networks, and reputation outside your current organization create a reference point that internal dysfunction cannot corrupt.

This layer takes longer to build but provides the most durable protection. Organizations change. Leaders change. Roles change. External credibility persists across all of them, providing both leverage within your current situation and options beyond it.

Documentation as Foundation

Credibility infrastructure requires evidence. When no manager tracks your contributions, you track them yourself. Professional discipline, not paranoia.

Documentation serves three functions in credibility architecture. First, it provides concrete material when opportunities arise — transforming vague claims into specific, credible statements. Second, it reveals patterns of problem-solving and value creation that individual contributions obscure. Third, it enables narrative control: your professional story built on evidence you hold, not memories others interpret.

The core practice: maintain an ongoing record of what you deliver, what problems you solve, and what value you create. (The full documentation protocol — what to capture, how to store it, when to surface it — is addressed in Chapter 7.)

A product manager keeps a simple running document of quarterly accomplishments: features shipped, problems solved, metrics improved. When an unexpected reorg creates a new leadership structure, she articulates her track record clearly to a new VP who has no prior context. Colleagues who kept no such records struggle to demonstrate their value and find themselves repositioned into less desirable roles.

Strategic Visibility Without Self-Promotion

The line between legitimate visibility and self-promotion is real.

The difference is orientation. Self-promotion centers on the professional: look at what I did. Strategic visibility centers on the work and the audience: here is information useful to you, here is context that helps the organization, here is visibility into outcomes that matter.

When Marcus Chen presents operational updates to senior leadership, he structures them around what executives need to know, not what makes him look good. The updates are genuinely informative. They solve a real problem for his audience, keeping them connected to a function they don't have time to monitor closely. That the updates also create visibility for Marcus and his team is a byproduct of providing value, not the transparent purpose.

"The moment it becomes about you, people sense it," Marcus observes. "They tune out, or worse, they start discounting what you say. When it's genuinely about information they need, they lean in. The visibility happens as a side effect of being useful."

Value first, visibility as byproduct — this separates sustainable credibility from the kind that erodes on contact. Professionals who build lasting reputations share credit broadly, frame updates in terms of organizational outcomes, and create natural visibility through genuine usefulness. They demonstrate value until it becomes obvious.

Credibility During Leadership Transitions

Distributed credibility proves most valuable during leadership transitions — when your direct manager leaves, is promoted, or is removed, and everything that existed only in their perception leaves with them. You start over, unless your credibility exists in channels beyond that single relationship.

Professionals with distributed infrastructure weather these transitions well. Lateral colleagues speak to their work. Senior leaders carry independent impressions. Documentation provides evidence that doesn't depend on anyone's memory. The transition becomes an opportunity rather than a reset.

Professionals with single-channel credibility face the opposite: everything built with the previous manager must be rebuilt with the new one. If the new manager arrives with their own preferred team, the single-channel professional may find themselves marginalized regardless of actual capability.

Elena has begun thinking about this since recognizing David's limitations. She doesn't know when David will leave or be moved, but she knows it will happen. When it does, she wants her credibility to stand independent of whatever narrative David would provide.

"I'm building relationships now that will matter when the situation changes," Elena explains. "Not because I'm planning to go around David. But because my reputation can't only exist in his head. It has to exist in enough places that one transition doesn't erase it."

The Reputation You're Building

What reputation are you actually building — given the signals you're sending and the channels through which those signals transmit?

Not what you intend or deserve. What you are building. The professional who works diligently but invisibly builds a reputation for invisibility. The one who delivers results but complains frequently builds a reputation as a complainer. The one who does excellent work but communicates only with their direct manager builds a reputation that depends entirely on that manager's perception.

Strategic Operators periodically audit their credibility infrastructure:

- Who beyond my direct manager can speak specifically to my contributions?
- What evidence exists of my work that doesn't depend on anyone's memory?
- If my manager left tomorrow, what would decision-makers know about me?
- What reputation am I building with the people who will determine my future opportunities?

The answers reveal gaps between intended reputation and actual reputation. Those gaps are the infrastructure that needs to be built.

The Long Game of Credibility

The Credibility Compound operates over months and years, not days and weeks.

Short-term thinking produces transactional behavior: seeking immediate visibility, chasing credit, building relationships only when something is needed. This approach is visible to others and damages the very credibility it attempts to build.

Long-term thinking produces investment behavior: building relationships before they're needed, creating value consistently rather than episodically, treating reputation as a multi-year asset rather than a quarterly metric. This is what compounds.

The professional who invests in credibility infrastructure during stable periods has assets to draw on during turbulent ones. The relationships built when nothing was at stake become valuable when everything is. The documentation maintained routinely becomes essential when specifically needed. The distributed credibility constructed over years holds when single channels fail.

The Strategic Operator builds credibility infrastructure before it's needed, because by the time it's needed, it's too late to start.

From Credibility to Sustainability

Infrastructure requires energy. And energy, under sustained dysfunction, is finite.

Visibility without stamina is a foundation that cracks under its own weight.

What follows is the resource beneath all infrastructure: professional energy, and what happens when it runs out.

Chapter 5: The Sustainability Equation

Performing at High Levels Without Burning Out

You come home and you have nothing left. Not because the work was hard — you can handle hard work. Because half of what exhausted you today was not your job. It was compensation for someone else's failure to do theirs.

Not exhaustion. Mis-allocated capacity — spent against unnecessary resistance, absorbed by the invisible second job of making dysfunction disappear.

The high performer's instinct is to absorb it. Fill the gaps. Protect the team. The instinct is understandable. It often produces short-term results. And it is, over any meaningful timeframe, unsustainable.

What happens after the instinct fails — and what replaces it — determines whether a career measured in decades remains viable.

The Hidden Costs of Compensation

When leadership fails, someone else pays the cost. Often, that someone is the competent professional directly below the failure.

The Conflict Avoider doesn't address the performance problem, so you work around the underperformer. The Absent Authority doesn't provide direction, so you create it yourself while lacking the positional power to enforce it. The Political Appointee commits to unrealistic timelines without consulting you, so you absorb impossible workloads to meet commitments you didn't make. The Micromanager Without Expertise demands explanations and updates that add hours to your week without adding value to your work.

Each of these compensations is individually manageable. Together, sustained over months and years, they constitute a second job: an invisible role that doesn't appear in your title, isn't reflected in your compensation, and generates no credit when performed well. The organization sees the output. It does not see the cost to the professional producing it.

The mechanism is self-reinforcing: leadership dysfunction persists precisely because competent people absorb it. The leader's inadequacy remains invisible to the organization because the professional below them makes it invisible. The worse the leadership, the more the professional compensates. The more they compensate, the less visible the leadership failure becomes.

Marcus Chen recognized this pattern three organizations ago, watching a colleague burn out under a Credit Absorber who appropriated every success while deflecting every failure.

"She was the best performer on the team," Marcus recalls. "And she was the one who left with nothing — exhausted, no credit, no advancement. The leader who caused it got promoted. The organization never understood what it lost because it never understood what she was contributing."

That observation shaped Marcus's approach. Excellence matters, but sustainability matters more. A career is measured in decades, not quarters.

Energy as Finite Resource

Professional energy is not unlimited. Most professionals behave as though it were.

They treat energy as infinitely renewable: something that will always be available tomorrow regardless of how much was spent today. They commit to unsustainable workloads, absorb unreasonable demands, and run deficits that compound until the system breaks down.

The breakdown, when it comes, rarely looks like dramatic collapse. More often it manifests as gradual erosion: declining quality, shortened patience, reduced capacity for strategic thinking, withdrawal from relationships that require effort. The professional still functions. They simply function at diminishing capacity, often without recognizing the decline.

Dysfunctional leadership manufactures all three accelerants simultaneously: ambiguous role expectations, low control over work conditions, and effort-reward imbalance. These three factors are not incidental observations. They are the most validated predictors of occupational burnout in decades of organizational health research. Dysfunctional leadership manufactures all three at once.

Energy is a finite resource. It must be allocated intentionally, monitored regularly, and replenished systematically.

Four categories of expenditure:

Core function work is the direct execution of your actual role: the deliverables, decisions, and outcomes you were hired to produce. Non-negotiable expenditure. Funded first.

Compensation work is energy spent filling gaps created by leadership dysfunction: the invisible second job described above. Some compensation work may be unavoidable, but it should be recognized as expenditure against a limited budget, not as normal operating cost.

Investment work is energy directed toward future returns: building relationships, developing capabilities, creating visibility, positioning for advancement. This expenditure compounds over time but requires current allocation.

Recovery is the energy required to restore capacity: rest, non-work activities, relationships outside the professional context. Not waste or indulgence. Essential maintenance.

Most professionals under-allocate to investment and recovery while over-allocating to compensation. They fund someone else's failures at the expense of their own future. The books balance quarterly. The trajectory bends downward.

Auditing the Cost

Before any allocation can be optimized, it must be observed. Most professionals dramatically underestimate how much energy they spend compensating for leadership dysfunction.

Track it for two weeks: every task, conversation, and commitment that exists only because leadership failed to perform their function. Professionals who estimate 10-15% of their effort goes to compensation routinely discover the actual figure is closer to 30-40%.

Elena Vasquez conducted this audit after a particularly exhausting quarter. She had delivered three major projects while David, her conflict-avoidant manager, had contributed almost nothing beyond vague approval. Her initial estimate was that compensation work represented perhaps 15% of her effort.

"The real number was closer to 35%," Elena admits. "I was creating the project plans David should have been providing. I was having the conversations with stakeholders David avoided. I was managing the conflicts he wouldn't touch. I knew I was doing extra work. I didn't know how much until I actually tracked it."

The audit changed how Elena thought about her situation. She wasn't just working hard. She was subsidizing David's role failure with resources that should have been building her own career.

That specificity — the shift from vague frustration to precise accounting — changes what becomes available.

Strategic Disengagement

What do you do with the information?

One option is to continue compensating indefinitely. This preserves short-term outcomes but guarantees long-term depletion. It is also invisible. The organization has no incentive to address dysfunction it doesn't perceive.

Another option is complete withdrawal, refusing all compensation work, letting leadership failure become visible through the consequences it produces. This has a certain logic to it. It is also career-risky. The professional who "lets things fail" may be blamed regardless of where the actual failure originated.

The Strategic Operator path lies between these extremes: **strategic disengagement**.

Strategic disengagement is the deliberate, calibrated reduction of compensation work to sustainable levels — a recognition that you cannot indefinitely fund someone else's role failure, and a determination to allocate finite resources toward your own trajectory rather than their deficit.

The practice requires distinguishing between compensation work that protects the organization and compensation work that protects the leader.

When Elena creates a project plan that David should have provided, she protects the organization; the project needs direction regardless of who provides it. When Elena shields David from consequences by never escalating his failures, she protects David; his inadequacy remains invisible because she makes it invisible.

Strategic disengagement reduces the second category while maintaining the first. The project still gets a plan. David's pattern of non-contribution becomes somewhat more visible. Elena preserves capacity for investment and recovery.

A product manager realizes she has been writing executive summaries for her Absent Authority director, documents he should produce but doesn't. Rather than continuing or refusing entirely, she shifts to providing bullet-point inputs that require his transformation into finished documents. The work product exists. His involvement is now required. Her time expenditure drops by hours weekly.

Make dysfunction visible without making yourself the casualty of that visibility. Strategic disengagement reduces compensation in ways that create natural consequences for leadership failure without creating attribution to professional insubordination.

Calibrating Boundaries

What disengagement reclaims, boundaries must protect. But they are not binary; they are calibrated.

Too rigid creates unnecessary conflict. The professional who refuses all requests outside their strict job description, who treats every boundary violation as a battle. This professional may preserve energy but damages relationships and trajectory. They are perceived as difficult, inflexible, not a team player.

Too flexible enables exploitation. The professional who accepts every request, absorbs every dysfunction, treats every "urgent" demand as equally deserving. This professional may be liked but is depleted. They become the default dumping ground for problems others don't want to handle.

The Strategic Operator calibrates boundaries along several lines.

Relationship capital considers who is making the request. Saying no to a peer you depend on for cross-functional success has different implications than saying no to someone you rarely interact with. Boundaries can flex more for relationships that matter to your trajectory.

Visibility impact considers who will observe the boundary. A request from senior leadership carries different boundary considerations than a request from a peer, not because hierarchy demands compliance but because perception among decision-makers affects trajectory.

Precedent effect considers what pattern the response establishes. Accepting an unreasonable request once may seem harmless. Accepting it consistently establishes an expectation that becomes progressively harder to change.

A senior analyst is asked to take notes in a leadership meeting, a task below her level but one that provides visibility with executives. She agrees, treating it as investment work. When the same request comes monthly, establishing a pattern where she has become the default note-taker, she declines the next instance while offering to help find an alternative solution. The initial flexibility served her; the emerging pattern would not.

The calibration is ongoing. Boundaries that made sense in one context require adjustment as situations change. The professional who maintains rigid boundaries from their first year through their tenth has failed to calibrate. The professional who maintains no boundaries has failed to sustain.

The Recovery Imperative

Energy that is spent must be restored. Not a concession to weakness — a condition of continued operation.

The professional under sustained leadership dysfunction faces particular recovery challenges. The stress is chronic, not acute; there is no clear endpoint after which recovery can begin. The dysfunction may pervade the work experience, making separation difficult. And the high performer's identity often resists the very concept of recovery, interpreting it as weakness or reduced commitment.

Effective recovery requires actual separation from the professional context — not just physical absence but mental disengagement. The professional who spends evenings ruminating about workplace dysfunction has not recovered; they have moved the depletion off-site.

What genuine recovery looks like varies individually. What matters is that it absorbs attention fully, exists outside the professional domain, and is protected.

Marcus maintains boundaries around recovery that might seem excessive to some colleagues. He does not check email after 7 PM or before 7 AM. He does not work weekends except in genuine emergencies, and he defines "emergency" narrowly. He takes his full vacation allocation every year.

"Some people read this as lack of commitment," Marcus acknowledges. "I read it as the reason I've been operating effectively for fourteen years. I've watched people who were more talented than me burn out and leave because they couldn't sustain. Being present at 80% capacity for two decades beats being present at 110% capacity for two years."

Heroic short-term effort cannot substitute for structural sustainability. The professional who depletes themselves in year three has no year ten.

When Sustainability Becomes Impossible

A harder truth: some situations cannot be made sustainable.

The dysfunction may be too severe, or the compensation required may exceed any reasonable energy budget. The leader may actively undermine every attempt to establish boundaries, and the organizational context may punish sustainability behaviors as insufficient commitment.

Strategic Operators recognize when sustainability requires not optimization but exit.

Preserving long-term career capacity sometimes requires leaving the situation that would destroy it. The professional who stays too long under unsustainable conditions damages not just current performance but future capability.

The signals that indicate sustainability failure include: persistent sleep disruption, physical health impacts, inability to recover even with time away, declining performance in areas previously strong, loss of engagement with work that previously mattered.

These signals should not be ignored or powered through. They indicate that the energy budget has been in deficit too long, and that continuing the current allocation pattern will produce lasting damage.

Elena has not reached this point; her situation under David is frustrating but not unsustainable. But she has observed colleagues who stayed too long, who believed they could outlast the dysfunction or that things would eventually improve.

"The ones who burned out all had the same story," Elena observes. "They thought they could handle it. They thought it was temporary. They thought leaving would be giving up. And then one day they couldn't function anymore, and it took them years to recover."

Knowing when to leave is as important as knowing how to stay.

Designing for Endurance

Sustainability is a design principle applied across professional operation.

It shapes how work is structured: building systems that don't require heroic effort, distributing load rather than concentrating it. It shapes how relationships are maintained: investing in connections that are reciprocal rather than extractive. It shapes how recovery is protected: treating energy restoration as infrastructure rather than luxury. And it shapes how decisions are evaluated: considering not just immediate outcomes but long-term capacity, asking not just *"can I do this?"* but *"can I sustain it?"*

The professional who designs for endurance may achieve less in any given quarter than the professional running at unsustainable intensity. Over a career, they will achieve more — because they will still be operating when the unsustainable professional has burned out.

From Stability to Influence

A professional who cannot regulate will struggle to influence. A professional who burns out has no trajectory.

Foundation secured. Now: the systems for strategic influence when leadership cannot or will not lead.

PART III: BUILD STRATEGIC INFLUENCE

Chapter 6: The Translation Layer

Communicating with Leaders Who Cannot Receive Direct Input

You see the system clearly. You are grounded within it. Now you need to communicate upward, and the person receiving that communication cannot process it in the form you would naturally deliver it.

This is the moment where most competent professionals stall. They know what needs to happen. They can articulate it with precision. They present clear analysis, sound reasoning, well-supported recommendations. And nothing changes. The leader doesn't act. Or acts in a direction that ignores the input entirely. Or agrees in the room and forgets by the following week.

The professional concludes, reasonably, that the leader doesn't listen. This conclusion is usually incomplete. The leader may not listen well. But the deeper problem is that the communication was delivered in a format the leader cannot receive. The content was sound. The translation was absent.

Translation — the skill of adapting communication to the receiver's capacity without sacrificing substance — is what separates influence from mere correctness.

The Assumption of Rational Reception

There is an assumption that runs deep among competent professionals: if I present information clearly and logically, it will be received clearly and logically.

This assumption works in environments where the receiver values clarity, processes logic, and acts on evidence. Many professional interactions operate this way. The assumption becomes habitual. And when it encounters a receiver who does not operate this way, the professional rarely questions the assumption. They question the receiver.

They are not wrong to question the receiver. But questioning the receiver does not produce outcomes. Adjusting the approach does.

Under competent leadership, communication is relatively straightforward. You present analysis. The leader evaluates it. Decisions follow from the quality of the input.

Under incompetent leadership, this relationship breaks. The quality of your input may have little bearing on the decision that follows. The leader may lack the domain knowledge to evaluate your analysis. They may filter it through insecurity, political calculation, or ego protection. They may agree with your assessment and still not act, because action requires capabilities they don't possess: confronting a peer, making a difficult trade-off, admitting uncertainty to their own leadership.

The competent professional who continues delivering excellent analysis to a leader who cannot process it is optimizing the input while ignoring the receiver. This is the communication equivalent of turning up the volume when the problem is the frequency.

The Nature of Translation

Translation is the adaptation of content — its format, framing, sequence, and emphasis — to match the receiver's processing capacity while preserving the substance of what needs to be communicated. The meaning stays intact. The delivery mechanism changes.

Many professionals resist the concept on principle. It feels like accommodation: like rewarding incompetence by adapting to it. And in a sense, it is accommodation. The question is whether that accommodation serves your objectives or undermines them.

The professional who refuses to translate preserves their sense of integrity. They also preserve their powerlessness.

The professional who translates preserves the substance while changing the wrapper. The recommendation gets implemented, the outcome moves closer to what it should be, and the professional's objective — which was never appreciation but outcomes — is achieved.

An engineering lead needs her VP to approve a resource allocation shift that will prevent a critical dependency failure in six months. The VP, a Peter Principle Promotion who rose through sales, doesn't process technical dependency analysis. Instead of presenting the systems architecture case, she frames the request around customer impact, language the VP understands intuitively. The resource shift is approved in one meeting. A colleague with an equally valid technical request, presented in technical terms, waits three months for a decision that never comes.

The Translation Layer Protocol

Translation under leadership constraints operates on four principles.

Diagnose the receiver before composing the message. The diagnostic work pays direct operational dividends here. The leader's archetype shapes what they can receive. A Conflict Avoider cannot process input that positions them to face confrontation. A Political Appointee filters everything through impact on their political standing. A Micromanager Without Expertise needs to feel involved in the decision process. A Peter Principle Promotion responds to frameworks from their area of prior competence. Diagnosis determines format.

Lead with what the receiver values, not what you value. The competent professional values accuracy, thoroughness, and analytical rigor. These are virtues. They are not universal reception frequencies. The leader who values political safety needs to hear how a recommendation protects their position. The leader who values simplicity needs the conclusion before the reasoning. The leader who values feeling in control needs a sense of ownership over the decision. Leading with what you value is self-expression. Leading with what they value is influence.

Reduce friction, not substance. Translation removes barriers between your input and the leader's action. Not by weakening the input, but by eliminating the elements that trigger resistance. Jargon the leader doesn't understand creates friction. Framing that implies criticism of their past decisions creates friction. Recommendations that require capabilities they lack create friction. The substance survives translation. The friction does not.

Calibrate depth to the decision required. Not every communication requires comprehensive analysis. A leader who needs to approve a resource shift needs enough context to feel confident in the decision, not a full accounting of every factor that informed the recommendation. Over-communicating to an under-processing receiver doesn't demonstrate thoroughness. It creates noise that obscures the signal.

Elena Vasquez has begun applying this protocol with David, her Conflict Avoider manager. Her previous approach, presenting clear analysis of problems and expecting David to act on them, failed consistently. The analysis required David to confront a situation, and confrontation is precisely what David cannot do.

Her translated approach looks different. When a resource conflict between two project streams requires David's intervention, Elena no longer frames it as a conflict requiring resolution. She frames it as a scheduling question: which project should receive the resource first? The decision is the same. The framing removes the interpersonal confrontation that would paralyze David.

"I stopped presenting problems and started presenting choices," Elena explains. "David can choose between options. He cannot walk into a conflict and resolve it. So I do the conflict resolution behind the scenes and give him a clean decision to make. He feels like he's managing. The problem actually gets solved."

The difference is visible in Elena's actual language.

Before she learned to translate, Elena's approach to a resource conflict sounded like this: "David, the Meridian and Cascade projects are competing for the same senior analyst for the next three weeks. Sarah can't support both timelines. We need you to decide which project takes priority, because the team leads are in disagreement and it's creating tension."

Every element of this communication is accurate. It is also precisely calibrated to trigger David's avoidance response. "Competing," "disagreement," "tension": the language signals interpersonal conflict requiring direct intervention. David hears the confrontation he would need to navigate and defers.

The translated version: "David, I want to confirm sequencing on two projects. Should Sarah finish the Meridian analysis first and shift to Cascade on the 15th, or reverse the order? Both paths work operationally — just need your preference on timing."

The substance is identical. But the framing has changed completely. Two viable options and a scheduling preference. David selects one in thirty seconds.

The conflict between the team leads — real and unresolved — Elena handles herself, offline, before bringing the clean choice to David.

"I do more work this way," Elena acknowledges. "I resolve the conflict, then present the outcome as logistics. But the alternative is presenting the real situation and watching nothing happen for two weeks."

Calibrating Influence

Not every situation warrants the same level of translational effort. Strategic Operators allocate influence resources along two dimensions: how receptive is the leader, and how high are the stakes?

High receptivity, low stakes: Direct communication works. The leader is open to input and the consequences are limited. State your recommendation clearly. Minimal translation required. Preserve your influence capital for situations that demand it.

High receptivity, high stakes: Direct but thorough. The leader is open to input but the decision carries significant consequences. Provide full context, address risks explicitly, and ensure the leader understands the implications. The receptivity is present. Honor it with the depth the stakes require.

Low receptivity, low stakes: Strategic patience. The leader is resistant to input and the decision doesn't significantly affect outcomes. This is where most influence capital is wasted. Professionals who fight every battle, who translate and frame and maneuver for decisions that barely matter, deplete themselves before the moments that count. Accept the imperfect outcome. Conserve capacity.

Low receptivity, high stakes: Maximum translation. The leader is resistant to input and the consequences are significant. This quadrant demands the full Translation Layer Protocol: careful diagnosis, receiver-centered framing, friction removal, calibrated depth. This is where translational skill pays its highest returns and where failure carries real cost.

Marcus Chen operates almost exclusively in the fourth quadrant with James. His Political Appointee leader is consistently low-receptivity on operational matters. James doesn't understand the function and doesn't prioritize understanding it. But the stakes of operational decisions are high. Marcus cannot afford to accept imperfect outcomes or to spend his influence on minor issues.

"I pick my moments," Marcus explains. "James makes bad operational calls weekly. I let most of them go — the team absorbs the inefficiency, and I don't spend capital fighting it. But when a decision will create real damage — losing a key person, committing to a timeline that will break the team, cutting a capability we can't rebuild — I go all in on translation. I frame it in terms James understands: how it affects his standing with the CEO, how it protects him from a problem he doesn't want to explain. The substance of what I need hasn't changed. The language has."

Influence capital is finite. The professional who spends it uniformly across all decisions will have none remaining when the decision matters most.

Translating by Archetype

The diagnostic taxonomy from Chapter 2 becomes directly operational here. Each archetype has a distinct reception pattern, and effective translation calibrates to that pattern.

The Peter Principle Promotion responds to input framed in the language of their prior competence. The former engineer who now leads a cross-functional team still processes engineering frameworks better than leadership ones. Translate into their native language when possible. They also respond to input that reduces their anxiety about operating beyond their depth: framing that makes the path forward feel manageable rather than overwhelming.

The Political Appointee filters everything through political impact. Translate into the language of stakeholder relationships, executive perception, and political protection. A recommendation that is operationally sound but politically risky will not survive their filter. A recommendation that is operationally sound and politically advantageous moves quickly.

The Absent Authority requires different translation: brevity that can penetrate their limited attention. Long analysis will never be read. The thirty-second summary with a clear action item has the best chance of producing a response. Documentation matters more here than elsewhere. The Absent Authority will forget verbal agreements, so the translation includes written confirmation.

The Micromanager Without Expertise needs to feel included in the process. Translation here means providing structured visibility (clear updates, defined checkpoints, transparent progress indicators) that satisfies their control needs without requiring their involvement in decisions they cannot usefully inform. Give them the dashboard. Protect the engine room.

The Credit Absorber requires translation that pre-positions credit. Frame recommendations so the leader can present them as their own without obscuring your contribution to those who matter. This is uncomfortable but strategically sound; the recommendation gets implemented, and the distributed credibility you have built ensures your contribution is recognized through other channels.

The Conflict Avoider requires translation that removes confrontational framing entirely. Present decisions as choices between options rather than problems requiring resolution. Eliminate language that implies someone is wrong or a situation is contentious. The Conflict Avoider will act on a framing that feels safe and avoid one that feels charged, regardless of the underlying substance.

The Ego Boundary

Translation frequently requires managing a dimension that has nothing to do with the substance of your communication: the leader's ego.

Many leadership failures are wrapped in ego protection. The Peter Principle Promotion who can't admit they're overwhelmed. The Political Appointee who can't acknowledge they don't understand the function. The Micromanager whose control needs mask insecurity. Input that threatens the ego, however unintentionally, triggers defensive responses that override rational processing.

Strategic Operators learn to deliver substantive input that navigates around the ego rather than through it.

This means framing recommendations as building on the leader's thinking rather than replacing it, even when the leader has contributed nothing. It means asking questions that lead to conclusions rather than stating conclusions that imply the leader should have reached them already. It means occasionally letting the leader believe an idea originated with them, when the origin matters less than the implementation.

Many professionals draw a line here. The discomfort is legitimate. But the Strategic Operator evaluates this trade-off against a specific question: does this serve my professional objectives? If the recommendation gets implemented, the project succeeds, and the outcome advances your trajectory, does it matter whether the leader believes the idea was theirs? Your credibility infrastructure exists precisely so that the people who matter know your contribution regardless of what the leader claims.

The ego boundary is about choosing which battles produce outcomes and which produce only the satisfaction of being right.

A finance director identifies a significant forecasting error that his VP missed during review. Rather than flagging the error directly (which would embarrass the VP in front of peers) he sends a private note suggesting they "pressure-test one assumption together before the board sees it." The VP catches the error in their joint review and presents the correction as due diligence. The forecast is accurate. The VP's ego is intact. The finance director's relationship with the VP strengthens. The outcome was never about credit for finding the error. It was about fixing it.

When Translation Fails

Translation is a capability, not a guarantee. There are situations where even skilled translation will not produce the desired outcome.

The leader may be so deeply incompetent that no framing can bridge the gap between what they can process and what the situation requires. The political dynamics may make the operationally correct decision impossible regardless of how it is presented. The leader may be actively hostile rather than merely limited, working against your interests rather than simply failing to serve them.

Strategic Operators recognize when translation has reached its limits. The signals are consistent: repeated attempts with adjusted framing produce no movement. The leader's pattern shows no variation regardless of approach. The gap between what is needed and what translation can achieve continues to widen.

When translation fails, the Strategic Operator faces a branching decision. Escalation — going above or around the leader — becomes a consideration, carrying its own costs and requirements. Documentation becomes critical, creating an evidence trail that protects the professional regardless of outcomes. And strategic patience may be necessary: accepting that some decisions will be wrong and positioning to manage the consequences rather than prevent the cause.

Translation is a high-return skill, not an omnipotent one.

The Identity Beneath the Skill

The professional who masters translation has moved from *"I communicate clearly and expect to be heard"* to *"I communicate strategically and take responsibility for being received."* This is not a compromise of standards. It is an expansion of capability.

This shift mirrors the broader Strategic Operator identity. The reactive professional expects the environment to accommodate their competence. The Strategic Operator adapts their approach to produce outcomes within the environment that actually exists.

Elena is beginning to internalize this. Her early frustration with David was rooted in an expectation that clear communication should produce clear action. That expectation was reasonable. It was also irrelevant. David's capacity to act on direct communication about conflict-laden situations is near zero, regardless of how clearly Elena presents her analysis. Adjusting the delivery to match David's capacity does not mean Elena's standards have dropped. It means her sophistication has increased.

"I used to think translating for David meant lowering myself," Elena reflects. "Now I see it differently. It's a harder skill than just being direct. Anyone can state the problem. Figuring out how to get the problem solved when the person above you can't hear it stated directly — that's a more advanced capability."

Translation is operational excellence in constrained environments. The constraint does not reduce the skill required. It increases it.

Translation establishes influence. What follows is the infrastructure that protects it: documentation systems that create evidence, preserve options, and ensure your professional contribution exists independent of any leader's memory or advocacy.

Chapter 7: Strategic Documentation

Documentation, Evidence, and Operational Foundation

Every Strategic Operator eventually encounters the same moment: a situation where something was agreed upon, a directive was given, a decision was made.

And now the account of what happened has shifted. The leader remembers differently. The priorities have changed without acknowledgment. The commitment that was clear last month has become ambiguous this month. And the professional who was present for the original conversation has nothing but their memory to reference.

Memory is unreliable. It is also unpersuasive. In organizational life, the version of events that exists in writing has structural advantage over the version that exists only in someone's recollection. This is true under competent leadership. Under incompetent leadership, where directives may be contradictory, accountability may be deflected, and credit may be misattributed, it is essential.

Documentation is the infrastructure that protects and enables strategic operation. Professional discipline, not defensiveness. The operational foundation that ensures your work, your agreements, and your contributions exist in forms that do not depend on any leader's memory, goodwill, or honesty.

Beyond Credibility: Documentation as Operating System

Documentation serves purposes beyond credibility that become critical under dysfunctional leadership.

Clarity and alignment are the first additional function. Under competent leadership, direction is usually consistent and commitments are honored. Under incompetent leadership, directions shift, priorities contradict, and verbal agreements dissolve. Documentation creates a reference point that holds — a stabilizer, not a weapon. When a leader's memory of a conversation differs from yours, the written confirmation you sent afterward functions as shared record.

Protection against attribution failure is the second. Documentation creates a factual record independent of anyone's narrative.

Operational continuity is the third. People leave. Leaders change. Reorganizations happen. The institutional memory that lives only in conversations and relationships walks out the door when those people depart. Documentation that captures decisions, rationale, and commitments preserves continuity across transitions, for you and for the organization.

These functions are interconnected. A single documented email confirming a project directive simultaneously serves clarity, protection, and continuity. Documentation, maintained consistently, operates as a professional system: not a collection of separate practices but an integrated infrastructure.

These functions become more critical in environments where leadership failure intensifies under pressure. Some leaders, when outcomes threaten their authority, reconstruct the sequence of events. Decisions they made become decisions they inherited. Directives they gave become suggestions that were misunderstood. This is an amplification of existing failure mechanisms: the Credit Absorber who also revises the record of contribution, the Conflict Avoider whose account of why a decision was deferred shifts with each retelling. Documentation does not prevent reconstruction. It creates a reference point that reconstruction cannot erase. The professional with a written record is preserving clarity in environments where clarity is structurally vulnerable.

The Documentation Protocol

Building documentation infrastructure requires a systematic approach. Ad hoc note-taking captures fragments. A structured protocol captures the patterns that matter.

Six categories of documentation, maintained consistently, create a comprehensive professional evidence base.

Stakeholder communications captured. Key interactions with stakeholders, including requests received, commitments made, expectations set, and feedback given, documented in retrievable form. This does not mean recording every conversation. It means confirming significant exchanges in writing. A brief email after a meeting: "Confirming my understanding from our discussion: the deliverable is X, the timeline is Y, and you'll provide Z by Friday." This serves alignment in the moment and evidence over time.

History of decisions and directives recorded. When leadership provides direction, particularly direction that may later shift or be denied, capture it. The Conflict Avoider who verbally approves a resource allocation but will not put it in writing gets a follow-up email: "Per our conversation, I'll proceed with moving Sarah to the compliance project for Q3." The Political Appointee who commits the team to an unrealistic deadline during an executive meeting gets a summary note: "Following today's discussion, confirming the timeline commitment of March 15. Below are the dependencies required to meet that date."

The goal is not to build a legal file. The goal is to create clarity where leadership creates ambiguity.

Instructions confirmed in writing. Verbal instructions are vulnerable to revision, reinterpretation, and selective recall. Written confirmations anchor them. When a directive arrives verbally, especially one you anticipate may later be contradicted or denied, confirm it in writing with a tone that frames the documentation as diligence, not distrust. "Want to make sure I have this right" is a phrase that costs nothing and protects everything.

Evidence of contributions preserved. Track what you deliver, what problems you solve, what outcomes you produce. Maintain this record independently — not in a system your manager controls, not in a format that depends on organizational tools that may change. A running document, updated regularly, that captures the substance of your professional contribution.

Lateral relationships documented. Cross-functional collaboration, peer feedback, joint problem-solving: these interactions build the distributed credibility that protects during leadership transitions. Documenting them does not mean keeping a relationship ledger. It means preserving evidence of collaborative work: shared project outcomes, emails acknowledging joint contributions, records of cross-functional impact. When your direct manager cannot speak to your value, these records provide alternative voices.

Deliverables and outcomes tracked. Not just what you delivered, but what it produced. The project was completed on time, but what business impact did it create? The process was redesigned, but what efficiency did it generate?

Outcomes are what organizations ultimately value. Tracking them transforms your record from a list of tasks completed to an account of value created.

The Practice of Professional Documentation

The documentation protocol is a framework. Making it operational requires embedding it into daily practice without creating a burden that consumes the energy it is meant to protect.

Effective documentation is lightweight and habitual. Five minutes after key interactions sending a brief confirmation email creates infrastructure. An hour each day meticulously recording every interaction creates a second job. The discipline is in the habit, not the volume.

Elena Vasquez has built this practice gradually since recognizing the single-channel vulnerability in her credibility infrastructure. Her approach is simple: after any meeting where David provides direction, makes a commitment, or agrees to a course of action, she sends a follow-up email summarizing her understanding. After any interaction with a stakeholder outside her direct team, she saves the relevant exchange. Once a month, she updates her private contribution record.

"It took me a while to make it automatic," Elena admits. "At first it felt like extra work — more effort on top of everything else. Now it's just how I close a conversation. The meeting ends, and I send the email. It takes two minutes. Those two minutes have already saved me twice."

The moments Elena references, situations where her documentation prevented a narrative from shifting beneath her, illustrate the asymmetric value of the practice. Documentation costs minutes to create. Its absence can cost weeks to remedy, if remedy is possible at all.

Tone and Positioning: The Adversarial Perception Problem

Documentation that appears adversarial creates the very conflict it is intended to manage.

The professional who sends confirmations that read like legal depositions — "Per your directive on March 3rd at 2:14 PM, you instructed me to..." — signals distrust. The leader feels surveilled. The relationship deteriorates. The documentation, intended as protection, becomes provocation.

Strategic Operators document with a tone that frames the practice as professionalism, not suspicion.

The confirmation email reads as diligence: "Want to make sure we're aligned — here's my understanding of next steps." The decision record reads as organizational discipline: "Capturing this for the team so everyone has the same reference point." The contribution log reads as preparation: "Pulling together my project summary for the quarterly review."

The content is the same. The framing determines how it is received.

Marcus Chen has refined this over years. His documentation practice is comprehensive: he maintains records of every significant commitment James makes, every resource allocation decision, every timeline agreement. But the documentation is positioned as operational management, not personal protection.

"I frame everything as being helpful," Marcus explains. "Summary emails after meetings aren't me covering myself. They're me making sure the division runs smoothly. Status updates to James aren't evidence collection. They're me keeping my leader informed. The documentation serves both purposes. But only one is visible."

The professional who documents well is simultaneously being a good operator and building a safety net. Both purposes are genuine. Only one is visible.

A program director inherits a project with a history of missed commitments from a predecessor. She begins each phase by sending her VP a brief "phase kickoff summary" outlining scope, dependencies, decision points, and what she needs from leadership to deliver on time. The tone is proactive and collaborative. When the VP later denies agreeing to a resource commitment that delays the project, the kickoff summary is there. The program director references it without accusation: "I want to revisit the resource plan from our phase kickoff — here's what we outlined." The conversation stays professional. The record holds.

What Not to Document

Professional documentation requires judgment about boundaries.

Do not document personal grievances as though they are professional records. The line between "my manager made a decision I disagree with" and "my manager failed to perform their function" matters. Documentation should capture observable professional events (decisions, directives, outcomes, contributions) not interpretive narratives about the leader's character or motivations.

Do not document private conversations between colleagues in ways that would damage trust if discovered. The lateral relationships that build distributed credibility depend on genuine trust. Documenting a peer's private frustration with leadership, for instance, would destroy the relationship if surfaced and would undermine the credibility infrastructure you are building.

Do not create documentation systems so elaborate that maintaining them becomes unsustainable. The protocol is a framework for what to capture, not a mandate for comprehensive surveillance of your professional environment. Capture what matters. Let the rest go.

Document events and agreements that have professional consequences if later disputed or forgotten. Everything else is noise.

Storage and Accessibility

Documentation that cannot be retrieved is documentation that does not exist.

Professional records should be stored in systems you control, not exclusively in organizational tools that may be revoked if you leave or are reorganized. Your private contribution log, your personal records of key decisions and directives, your evidence of outcomes. These should exist in a location that survives any single organizational change.

This does not mean removing proprietary information from organizational systems. It means maintaining your own records of your own contributions, your own confirmations of agreements, and your own tracking of professional activity, in formats and locations that remain accessible regardless of what happens organizationally.

If you lost access to all organizational systems tomorrow, could you reconstruct a credible account of your professional contributions, the commitments made to you, and the decisions that shaped your work? If the answer is no, your documentation infrastructure has a single point of failure.

When Documentation Becomes Essential

Documentation operates as background practice until specific conditions make it foreground necessity.

When leadership begins contradicting prior commitments — denying agreements, redistributing accountability, reconstructing timelines — documentation becomes the stabilizing reference. The professional with records can respond calmly: "I want to make sure I'm not misremembering — let me check my notes from our March meeting." The professional without records can only assert their memory against the leader's, a contest they are structurally positioned to lose.

When organizational change is approaching (restructuring, leadership transitions, reductions) documentation of contributions and outcomes becomes the evidence that determines positioning. Decision-makers evaluating who is essential will rely on available evidence. Professionals who have maintained that evidence have an advantage that cannot be manufactured retroactively.

When a situation may require formal intervention (when dysfunction reaches a level demanding escalation) documentation provides the factual foundation. Vague complaints about leadership dysfunction carry little weight. Specific, documented patterns carry substantially more. The professional who has maintained records does not need to reconstruct months of history under pressure. The history is already captured.

Elena has not yet needed her documentation for escalation purposes. But she has noticed something the practice provides independent of any crisis: peace of mind. The anxiety of operating under unreliable leadership diminishes when you know that your version of events has an evidence base. You are not depending on David's memory to confirm what he agreed to. You are not depending on David's willingness to attribute credit accurately. The record exists. It is yours.

"The documentation isn't about David," Elena observes. "It's about me. It's about knowing that no matter what happens — if David leaves, if there's a reorg, if someone questions my contribution — I have what I need. I'm not dependent on anyone else's version of what happened."

Infrastructure Complete

There remains a category of situation that translation and documentation cannot address: when dysfunction exceeds what can be navigated from below, and the gap between what the situation requires and what your position allows becomes untenable.

That moment calls for a different calculus.

Next: the highest-stakes decision in the Strategic Operator's repertoire.

Chapter 8: The Escalation Calculus

When to Go Over, Around, or Through

At some point, every professional navigating leadership dysfunction considers the same thought: I should go above them.

The frustration has accumulated. The translation efforts have produced limited results. The documentation paints a clear picture of a pattern that isn't improving. Something has to change, and the tools available within the current reporting relationship seem exhausted.

The instinct to escalate feels like progress. After months or years of navigating dysfunction from below, the idea of bringing the problem to someone with the authority to address it carries enormous appeal. The assumption is that the system has a correction mechanism and that triggering it is simply a matter of presenting the evidence.

It might. The question is not whether escalation is possible, but whether escalation, in this specific situation, is strategically sound: whether the probable outcomes justify the certain costs, and whether the timing, positioning, and evidence align to give the intervention its best chance of producing change.

The Asymmetry of Escalation

The first reality of escalation is structural asymmetry: the professional who escalates bears disproportionate risk compared to the leader being escalated about. The imbalance is architectural.

The leader occupies a higher organizational position. They have, by definition, more political capital, more relationships with the people who will judge the escalation, and more influence over how the situation is framed after the fact. The leader who learns they've been escalated about can retaliate through performance evaluations, project assignments, access restriction, or subtle reputational damage. And because they hold positional authority, their retaliation may be difficult to distinguish from normal management decisions.

The escalating professional, meanwhile, enters the process with their own credibility on the line. The decision-maker receiving the escalation must evaluate not just the leader's behavior but the professional's motives. Are they raising a legitimate concern, or are they a disgruntled employee who couldn't handle a difficult relationship? The framing often favors the leader, because organizations are predisposed to trust hierarchical authority over complaints from below. The predisposition is measurable. Employees who raise formal concerns about superiors face retaliation in roughly one out of five cases — even when the complaint is substantiated. The asymmetry is not perception. It is actuarial.

This asymmetry does not mean escalation is never warranted. It means escalation is never free. The professional who escalates spends political capital, assumes risk, and accepts that the outcome may not be what they intended. Escalation is an investment decision, not an act of protest.

Marcus Chen understands this cost structure intimately. His situation with James, a Political Appointee who doesn't understand the function he nominally leads, presents a textbook case for escalation. James makes commitments without operational understanding. He creates problems Marcus must solve. The dysfunction is documented and persistent.

Marcus has not escalated.

"James reports to the CEO," Marcus explains. "The CEO put him there. Escalating to the CEO about James is escalating to the person who made the decision I'm questioning. The asymmetry isn't just organizational — it's personal. The CEO would have to admit a mistake to act on my complaint. That's not a calculation that favors me."

Marcus has weighed the probable outcome of escalation against its certain costs and concluded that his strategic objectives are better served by other approaches — for now. The calculus could change. But at this moment, escalation would cost more than it could plausibly produce.

The Risk Calculus

The decision to escalate requires structured evaluation, not accumulated frustration reaching a tipping point.

The risk calculus evaluates five dimensions before any high-stakes professional action.

Probability of success. What is the realistic likelihood that escalation will produce the desired outcome? Not the hoped-for outcome, the probable one. This requires assessing who will receive the escalation, what they are likely to do with it, and what constraints they operate under. A skip-level leader already aware of the problem and declining to act is unlikely to act because you surfaced it again. An HR department lacking authority to override senior leadership cannot produce outcomes requiring that override. Probability assessment demands honest evaluation of the system you're in, not the system you wish existed.

Cost of success. Even when escalation produces its intended result, there are costs. The leader who is reprimanded, reassigned, or removed may have allies. The professional who triggered the intervention may be perceived as a threat by others in the hierarchy. The team dynamics shift. The professional's reputation as "someone who escalates" follows them, for better or worse. Success does not mean cost-free.

Cost of failure. When escalation does not produce change — and this is common — the professional's position is typically worse than before. The leader now knows they've been escalated about. The relationship is damaged in ways that may be irreparable. The decision-maker who heard the escalation and chose not to act has implicitly endorsed the current arrangement. The professional has spent capital and received nothing in return.

Cost of inaction. This is the dimension most often overlooked. What happens if you don't escalate? Does the situation deteriorate further? Does your career sustain ongoing damage? Are other people being harmed by the dysfunction? The cost of inaction is not zero; if it were, escalation wouldn't be under consideration. Quantifying this cost as clearly as you quantify the cost of action prevents the calculation from defaulting to risk avoidance.

Reversibility. Can the escalation be undone if it goes wrong? In most cases, the answer is no. Once you have gone above your manager or filed a complaint with HR, that action exists in the organizational record, formally or informally. This irreversibility is what makes escalation fundamentally different from the other tools in the Strategic Operator's repertoire. Translation can be adjusted. Documentation can be maintained quietly. Escalation, once initiated, cannot be recalled.

The Calculus is not a formula that produces a clear answer. It is a framework that forces clarity about the variables that matter. Professionals who escalate without conducting this assessment are making high-stakes decisions based on emotional pressure rather than strategic evaluation.

Skip-Level Escalation

Going above your manager to their manager is the most common form of escalation, and among the most delicate.

The skip-level leader occupies a complex position in this dynamic. They may be genuinely unaware of the dysfunction below them. They may be partially aware but not sufficiently motivated to intervene. They may be fully aware and actively choosing not to act, for reasons invisible from your vantage point: political considerations, plans already in motion, constraints you cannot see.

Approaching a skip-level leader about their direct report requires precision. The framing must be professional, not emotional. The evidence must be specific, not general. The focus should be on business impact, what the dysfunction costs the organization, rather than personal grievance, which is easy to dismiss.

The most effective skip-level escalations present documented patterns rather than isolated incidents. They focus on organizational harm rather than personal frustration. They offer the skip-level leader a way to address the situation without public confrontation. And they do not require the skip-level leader to choose between you and their direct report, a choice they will almost never resolve in your favor.

The most strategically effective escalations often don't look like escalations at all. They frame the problem as organizational rather than personal, propose solutions rather than accusations, and give decision-makers a path of action that doesn't require them to take sides.

Not all situations permit this kind of framing. Some dysfunction is personal rather than processual. Some leaders are the problem, not the process. But where indirect escalation is possible, it typically produces better outcomes at lower cost than direct confrontation.

When the threshold is crossed, the documentation is what makes escalation viable.

A senior project manager, eighteen months under a director who routinely commits the team to client timelines without consulting delivery leads, reaches her threshold when a commitment creates genuine organizational risk: a contractual delivery date the team cannot meet without sustained overtime that will break retention. She has documented every instance.

Her documentation file contains fourteen entries over eleven months. Each follows the same format: date, commitment made, who made it, who was consulted (consistently no one on the delivery side), downstream impact, and resolution. The pattern is legible at a glance. This is not a collection of grievances. It is an operational record.

Her escalation takes the form of a meeting request to the VP of operations:

"Hi Michael — I'd like to discuss a delivery risk pattern that I think needs your visibility. Over the past eleven months, we've had fourteen instances where client commitments were made before delivery validation. I've been tracking these and managing the downstream impact, but the most recent commitment creates a timeline risk I can't absorb without significant team impact. I have documentation I'd like to walk you through. Would you have thirty minutes this week?"

The email does not name the director. It does not use words like "complaint," "problem," or "concern about leadership." It frames a business risk, offers evidence, and requests a conversation. The VP agrees to the meeting. The documentation speaks for itself.

The outcome: a process change requiring delivery sign-off before client commitments. The director's behavior is constrained. The project manager's professional relationship with the VP is strengthened rather than damaged. The escalation succeeded because the evidence was systematic, the framing was organizational, and the request was specific.

HR: What It Is and What It Isn't

Human Resources is among the most misunderstood functions in organizational life, and that misunderstanding leads professionals to engage with it in ways that produce frustration rather than resolution.

HR serves the organization. This is not cynicism. It is structural reality. HR's primary function is managing organizational risk: legal exposure, regulatory compliance, talent retention at scale, employment practices that protect the company. Individual employee advocacy exists within this framework, but it is not the framework's purpose.

This means HR's response to your escalation will be shaped by the organization's interests, not yours. When those interests align (when your complaint also represents organizational risk) HR can be a powerful mechanism. When they diverge (when addressing your complaint would create political difficulty, expose leadership failures that senior executives prefer to manage quietly, or require action against someone with significant organizational capital)

HR's response will reflect that divergence. There is also a structural bias toward management incumbents: replacing a leader carries higher organizational cost than retaining a dissatisfied individual contributor, and HR's calculus reflects that arithmetic.

HR has constraints you cannot see. The HR professional hearing your complaint may be sympathetic and still unable to act. They may face political pressure from above. They may know things about the situation they cannot share. They may have received similar complaints and be building a case that takes time. Or they may have assessed that the situation, while frustrating, does not meet the threshold for organizational intervention. Their constraints are real even when they are invisible.

HR processes are not courts. They do not operate on principles of fairness as you might define them. There is no neutral judge. There is no burden of proof standard. There is no guarantee of a proportionate response. HR investigations serve organizational interests, and the outcomes reflect organizational priorities.

None of this means HR should be avoided. It means HR should be engaged with clear-eyed expectations.

Engaging HR

Four questions structure the evaluation of whether and how to engage HR.

Is this an HR matter? Not all leadership dysfunction falls within HR's scope. General incompetence (a leader who is bad at their job but does not violate policy) is typically not something HR can address. Performance management of leaders is their manager's responsibility, not HR's. Situations that are HR matters include: policy violations, harassment, discrimination, retaliation, safety concerns, and ethical breaches. If the dysfunction does not involve a policy violation or legal exposure, HR's ability to act is limited regardless of how well you present your case.

Do you have documentation? HR processes depend on evidence. Vague assertions about leadership problems ("my manager doesn't support me," "my manager takes credit for my work") are difficult for HR to act on even when they are true. Specific, documented instances (dates, communications, patterns, business impact) provide the material HR needs to investigate and act. The documentation protocol exists partly for this purpose: if escalation becomes necessary, the documentation is already in place.

What outcome are you seeking? This question forces precision. Are you seeking investigation of a specific violation? Mediation of a relationship? Transfer to a different team? Removal of the leader? Each outcome has a different probability of success and requires different evidence. The professional who engages HR with a clear objective is more likely to receive a useful response than the one who arrives with a general complaint hoping HR will determine the solution.

What is your fallback if HR cannot help? HR engagement does not guarantee resolution. Before initiating the process, the Strategic Operator identifies what they will do if the outcome is unsatisfying. Internal transfer? External exit? Continued navigation with documentation? Having a fallback prevents the professional from being strategically stranded after an unsuccessful HR engagement.

The Aftermath

Escalation produces consequences regardless of outcome. Success changes the environment in complex ways: allies of the departed leader recalibrate, colleagues adjust their own risk assessments, and the professional's reputation shifts toward "courageous" or "dangerous" or both. Failure deteriorates the operating position: the leader now carries the knowledge of being escalated about, trust is diminished on both sides, and exit may become the only remaining strategic option.

In both cases, the same resource has been consumed. Political capital has been spent. The professional's name is now permanently associated with the escalation in the minds of decision-makers.

Marcus weighs this permanence against his other options. Three years from a significant equity vesting event, with a Political Appointee leader whose sponsor is the CEO, the calculation is complex. Escalation that fails costs him the equity. Escalation that succeeds, if James were reassigned, might create a better operating environment but would also mark Marcus as someone who challenged the CEO's judgment.

"I run the numbers quarterly," Marcus says. "Not literally — but I reassess. Is the cost of staying under James greater than or less than the value of the equity and the risk of escalation? Right now, the answer is clear. But I track it. Because the variables change. James could get worse. The equity could become less significant relative to what I'm losing. The CEO could leave, changing the political protection entirely. I don't escalate today. That doesn't mean I never will."

When Not to Escalate

The Strategic Operator's default is not escalation. It is navigation.

Escalation is warranted when the dysfunction produces harm that cannot be mitigated through communication, documentation, and strategic positioning — when the cost of inaction exceeds the cost of action, or when policy violations and ethical breaches make inaction untenable.

Frustration alone does not meet this threshold. Neither does incompetence. Organizational systems are not designed to receive the complaint that your leader is bad at their job, however true it may be.

The distinction is between situations that are navigable and situations that are not. Navigable dysfunction is managed through the tools already established: diagnosis, stability, credibility, sustainability, translation, documentation. They do not eliminate dysfunction. They enable operation within it while protecting trajectory.

Non-navigable dysfunction requires intervention from above or exit from below. The signs include: documented deterioration that communication cannot reverse, harm to your career that positioning cannot offset, ethical violations you cannot in good conscience accommodate, or health impacts that sustainability practices cannot manage.

Elena has considered escalation about David. She has the documentation. She can articulate the pattern. But she has also conducted the risk calculus.

"David isn't causing damage that I can't manage," Elena assesses. "He's frustrating. He limits what I can accomplish through his channel. But I've built other channels. I've learned to translate for him. I document everything. My career isn't stalled — it's moving, just not as fast as it would under better leadership. Escalating about David would spend enormous capital for what? Getting him replaced with someone who might be worse? David's flaw is avoidance. That's manageable. A Credit Absorber or a hostile Micromanager would be harder."

This assessment reflects diagnostic maturity. The tools she has built — translation, documentation, distributed credibility — have reduced the cost of David's dysfunction to a level she can sustain while building trajectory. Escalation would introduce risks that exceed the benefits.

The Strategic Operator escalates when the calculus demands it. Not before.

The Escalation Resource

Escalation is a resource in the same sense that political capital is a resource: finite, difficult to rebuild once spent, and most valuable when deployed at the moment of greatest leverage.

The professional who escalates frequently, who brings every frustration to a skip-level leader and engages HR over every conflict, depletes this resource until it carries no weight. Their escalations become background noise, easily dismissed by the very decision-makers they are trying to reach.

The professional who never escalates, who absorbs every dysfunction and treats escalation as something that is never warranted, fails to deploy a resource that exists for precisely the situations they are enduring. Their restraint may be admirable. It may also be enabling the very patterns they wish would change.

The Strategic Operator holds escalation in reserve, maintains the documentation that would support it, and deploys it when — and only when — the calculus justifies the cost. A high-stakes intervention that can alter the trajectory of a situation at the right moment, and a career at the wrong one.

The tools for strategic influence now established, we turn to the wider field: organizational dynamics, political systems, and the career engineering that transforms a stabilized professional into one whose trajectory is self-directed.

PART IV: ENGINEER YOUR TRAJECTORY

Chapter 9: Political Fluency

Navigating Organizational Dynamics Without Compromising Integrity

The work should speak for itself. This is the conviction of a professional who takes pride in staying above office politics, who focuses on delivery, who does not engage in the maneuvering and alliance-building that others spend time on.

The conviction is sincere.

It also has a cost.

The professional who refuses to engage with organizational politics does not escape politics. They simply operate within political systems without understanding them.

Political fluency — the capacity to understand and operate within organizational power dynamics without abandoning professional integrity — is organizational literacy. Refusing to acquire it does not preserve integrity. It sacrifices leverage.

The Resistance to Political Engagement

The resistance is understandable. Professionals who have invested in capability and delivery reasonably expect those investments to determine trajectory.

But organizations are human institutions operating according to human dynamics: relationships, perception, reciprocity, trust, allegiance. These dynamics shape decisions as much as competence does. Sometimes more. Acknowledging this is not abandoning values. It is seeing the system as it operates and positioning within it accordingly.

The cost of political naïveté is not abstract. It shows up in specific, measurable consequences: the promotion that goes to a less qualified peer who built better relationships with decision-makers. The project assignment that goes to someone who positioned themselves effectively while you waited to be noticed. The reorganization that places you outside the new power structure because no one in that structure knew your name.

Elena Vasquez experienced this cost directly. Her first passed-over promotion (the one that preceded her recognition of the visibility trap) was a political outcome. The colleague who was promoted had invested in relationships with the executive team. Elena had invested in project delivery. Both investments were legitimate. Only one produced advancement.

"I thought politics was the problem," Elena reflects now. "What I didn't see was that politics is just how organizations make decisions when there isn't a formula. If you don't participate, you don't get considered. Not because the system is corrupt. Because the system runs on relationships, and if you aren't in the relationship, you aren't in the system."

Political Awareness vs. Political Manipulation

Political awareness is understanding how power, influence, and decisions operate in your organization: who makes decisions, who influences decision-makers, what relationships shape resource allocation, and how information flows through formal and informal channels. This is organizational literacy. It does not require you to do anything manipulative. It simply means seeing the system clearly.

Political manipulation is using that understanding to advance your interests at others' expense, through deception, sabotage, information hoarding, or strategic betrayal. It means treating relationships as purely instrumental, people as means to ends, and organizational trust as a resource to be exploited.

The line between these two is real, and Strategic Operators respect it.

Awareness means understanding that a senior leader's opinion carries weight in promotion decisions and building a genuine professional relationship with them. Manipulation means cultivating that relationship through false agreement, strategic flattery, or undermining competitors for their attention.

Awareness means knowing that a reorganization is being discussed and positioning yourself for the new structure. Manipulation means acquiring confidential information through deception and using it to disadvantage peers.

Awareness means understanding what decision-makers value and framing your contributions in terms that resonate with them. Manipulation means fabricating contributions or claiming credit for others' work to match those values.

Most professionals recognize the line when they see it. The difficulty is accepting that political awareness, on its own, is legitimate and necessary. Political skill is an established professional competency that predicts career advancement and organizational effectiveness independent of manipulative behavior. The evidence is substantial and the distinction is important: political skill — social awareness, networking, interpersonal influence — predicts career outcomes across dozens of studies, and it is empirically distinct from manipulation. The two look different, produce different results, and develop through different behaviors.

Formal and Informal Power

Every organization operates on two power structures simultaneously.

Formal power is what the organizational chart describes: reporting lines, titles, designated authority. The VP has authority over directors. The director has authority over managers. Formal power determines who can approve budgets, make hiring decisions, and sign off on strategic direction. It is visible, documented, and sanctioned.

Informal power is what the organizational chart does not describe: the relationships, reputations, and accumulated influence that shape decisions independent of formal authority. The senior individual contributor who has the CEO's ear carries more influence than their title suggests. The executive assistant who controls access to the C-suite has gatekeeping power that no org chart reflects. The mid-level manager who has built deep cross-functional relationships can mobilize resources that their formal authority alone would not command.

Organizational decisions — particularly decisions about people, opportunities, and resources — are shaped by both structures. Formal power determines who has the authority to decide. Informal power determines who influences the deciding.

The professional who understands only formal power is perpetually surprised when outcomes don't match hierarchical logic. The professional who understands both structures sees how decisions actually get made, and can position themselves within the real system, not just the official one.

A director of engineering wants to launch a platform initiative that requires cross-divisional support. She has formal authority within her division but none across divisions. She identifies three people whose informal influence will determine whether the initiative gains traction: a product VP who has the CEO's trust on strategic direction, a senior architect respected across all technical teams, and an operations lead whose cooperation is practically essential. She invests in each relationship before proposing the initiative formally, understanding the technical concerns, aligning on shared objectives, addressing logistical dependencies. When the proposal reaches the executive team, three influential voices are already aligned. The formal decision follows the informal groundwork.

Mapping the Political Landscape

The political map tracks the power dynamics that affect your professional trajectory. It maps five elements.

Decision-makers are the people who hold actual authority over outcomes that matter to you: promotions, project assignments, resource allocation, organizational positioning. They may or may not be your direct manager. They may be your manager's manager, a peer of your manager in another function, or an executive whose involvement in decisions about your level is intermittent but decisive. Identifying who actually decides (as opposed to who you assume decides) is the first step.

Influencers are the people who shape decision-makers' thinking without holding formal decision authority. They might be trusted advisors, long-tenured peers, or professionals whose judgment carries informal weight. A decision-maker who consults three people before making promotion decisions has three influencers whose perception of you matters as much as the decision-maker's own.

Gatekeepers control access to information, decision-makers, and opportunities. A chief of staff who manages an executive's calendar, a program manager who assigns high-visibility projects — their cooperation enables access. Their indifference prevents it.

Allies share your interests, value your work, or have reason to support your advancement. They may be peers who benefit from your success, mentors who have invested in your development, or leaders who have observed your capability and are inclined to advocate. Allies are not permanent or unconditional. They are professionals whose interests align with yours in specific contexts.

Dynamics are the relationships between these actors: the alliances, tensions, rivalries, and histories that shape how they interact. Understanding that two senior leaders are in competition for the same resources explains why supporting one may alienate the other. Recognizing that a decision-maker relies heavily on a particular influencer tells you where to direct relationship-building effort.

The map evolves as people move, relationships shift, and dynamics change. Strategic Operators update it through attentive observation of how decisions are made, how information flows, and how power is exercised.

Elena builds her map by observation, not interrogation.

She starts with the question the map demands first: who actually decides whether she advances? The answer is not David. David submits the recommendation, but Elena has learned through careful attention that promotion decisions at her level are made in a quarterly leadership review chaired by the division VP. David participates, but so do three other directors and the VP's chief of staff.

This changes everything. David is a channel, not the decision-maker.

The next question: who influences the VP's assessment of candidates? Elena observes. She notices which names the VP references in all-hands meetings. She notes which directors the VP consults before announcing organizational changes. She identifies two: the director of product, who has a long working history with the VP, and the chief of staff, who prepares the briefing materials for every leadership review.

She does not ask anyone directly about the power structure. She listens. In cross-functional meetings, she notes who speaks and who is deferred to. In casual conversations, she asks neutral questions: "How did the decision on the Q3 initiative come together?" "Who was involved in shaping the new org structure?" These are professional curiosity, not intelligence gathering. The answers build her map.

The testing is equally calibrated. Elena volunteers for a cross-functional workstream that places her in regular contact with the product director — not to perform, but to create the conditions where her work is observed by someone whose perception matters. She does not mention her career goals. She delivers well. The observation happens naturally.

Within three months, Elena has a working map: two decision-influencers she barely knew existed, a gatekeeper whose briefing materials shape every promotion discussion, and a clearer understanding of which relationships will matter when the decision window opens. None of this required a single political maneuver. It required attention.

Reading the Room You're Not In

Consequential decisions about your career are made in conversations you are not part of.

Promotion discussions happen among leaders in meetings you don't attend. Resource allocation decisions are shaped by relationships you may not see. Your name is mentioned, or not mentioned, in contexts where you cannot advocate for yourself.

Distributed credibility, strategic visibility, and political awareness function as an integrated system. Each ensures your interests are represented in rooms you cannot enter.

Marcus Chen operates with this awareness constantly. He knows that decisions about his division's budget are not made in his budget meetings with James. They are made when James meets with the CFO and the CEO, conversations Marcus has no direct access to. He knows that James, a Political Appointee, will represent the division's needs only to the extent that doing so serves his own standing.

"I cannot be in those rooms," Marcus acknowledges. "But I can influence what James carries into them. And I can ensure that the CFO has an independent impression of our operational performance through the quarterly reports I structure for his team. When James undersells us — which he does, because he doesn't understand what we do — the data exists in another channel."

Political fluency in practice: understanding where decisions are made, who makes them, what influences them, and how to ensure your interests are represented even when you are absent.

Building Political Capital

Political capital is built through patterns, not transactions.

Reliability is the foundation. Consistent delivery on commitments builds political capital with everyone you interact with. Decision-makers and influencers trust professionals they can rely on. Every other form of political capital rests on this floor.

Reciprocity amplifies it. Genuine help without immediate expectation of return creates a network of positive obligations. The peer you helped with a complex problem remembers when your name comes up in a staffing discussion. The executive you provided with useful information outside your normal scope remembers when promotion candidates are reviewed. It compounds over time.

Strategic alignment concentrates it. Political capital invested broadly has diffuse returns. Political capital concentrated on relationships that connect to your trajectory has focused returns. This does not mean ignoring people who cannot help you. It means being intentional about where you invest your deepest relationship-building effort: the decision-makers, influencers, and allies whose perception of you most directly affects your opportunities.

A compliance analyst identifies that her skip-level leader is focused on audit readiness; it is his primary performance objective for the year. Without being asked, she prepares a brief analysis of three areas where the team's documentation has gaps that an auditor would flag. She sends it to her manager and copies the skip-level leader with a note: "Thought this might be useful for the audit prep initiative." The analysis takes her two hours. The skip-level leader now knows her name, associates her with proactive value, and has independent evidence of her capability. When a senior analyst position opens three months later, her name comes up in a room she's never entered.

The Ethics of Political Operation

Political fluency without ethical boundaries is manipulation. The Strategic Operator operates within boundaries that preserve integrity while enabling effective navigation.

Do not misrepresent. Framing your contributions effectively is legitimate. Fabricating or exaggerating them is not. The line is whether someone who investigated the claim would find it accurate.

Do not sabotage. Competing for opportunity is legitimate. Undermining a peer's reputation or work to create competitive advantage is not. The line is whether you are building your own position or damaging someone else's.

Do not betray confidence. Using information shared in trust (from peers, from mentors, from any professional relationship) as political currency destroys the relationships that generate long-term political capital. Short-term gain from betrayed confidence is always a net negative.

Do not build alliances against people. Building alliances around shared interests is legitimate. Building alliances organized primarily around opposition to a colleague is factional behavior that damages organizational culture and eventually damages the professional who initiates it.

These boundaries are strategic, not just ethical. Manipulation may produce short-term wins but builds a reputation that compounds negatively. Clean political navigation builds trust that compounds positively. Over a career, the differential is not close.

Elena is testing these boundaries as she develops political awareness. She has begun building relationships with stakeholders outside her immediate reporting line: skip-level leaders, cross-functional peers, professionals whose influence connects to her trajectory. The relationships are genuine. She is not performing interest she doesn't feel. She is investing in connections she should have built years ago.

"The difference between what I'm doing now and what I used to think of as 'politics' is that I'm not pretending anything," Elena explains. "I'm not flattering people I don't respect. I'm not agreeing with things I disagree with. I'm building real professional relationships with people whose work intersects mine. I just wasn't doing that before because I thought the work would be enough."

From Fluency to Visibility

The map alone does not create movement. Visibility, leverage, and positioning translate awareness into advancement.

That convergence is designed.

The landscape is mapped. What follows is the engineering.

Chapter 10: The Visibility Imperative

Leverage, Reputation Capital, and Promotion Readiness

Most high performers believe promotion is primarily a function of performance. Do excellent work. Build capability. Deliver results. The organization will eventually recognize and reward it.

This belief is approximately half correct. Job performance accounts for a modest portion of the variance in who actually advances. Sponsorship, visibility to decision-makers, and organizational fit explain equal or greater variance. Performance gets you considered. Everything else determines whether you are selected.

Performance is necessary. Without it, nothing else matters. But performance alone does not produce advancement, particularly under leadership that cannot or will not represent your value to the people who make promotion decisions. The gap between what you contribute and what the organization recognizes you for — the performance-perception gap — does not close itself. It must be engineered closed.

The Strategic Operator builds the systems that produce recognition.

How Promotion Decisions Actually Work

Promotion decisions in most organizations involve five factors, and professionals who understand only one of them are structurally disadvantaged.

Performance is the baseline. You must have a credible record of contribution. Without it, no amount of visibility or positioning will sustain advancement. But performance is table stakes. It gets you considered, not selected.

Perception determines how decision-makers assess your readiness: the picture of you assembled from observation, reputation, and narrative. Two professionals with identical performance records may generate entirely different perceptions. The difference is not in what they do but in what decision-makers believe about what they do.

Sponsorship is advocacy in rooms you cannot enter. Someone with credibility and influence spends their own political capital to make the case for your advancement. Under functional leadership, your direct manager serves this function. Under dysfunctional leadership, this channel may be weak, absent, or counterproductive.

Timing is the organizational context surrounding the decision. Budget cycles, structural openings, strategic shifts, and leadership changes all affect when opportunities exist and who is positioned to capture them. The professional who is ready when the opening appears advances. The professional who becomes ready six months later waits for the next cycle, which may not come.

Risk perception is the factor most professionals overlook entirely. Decision-makers evaluating promotions are not only assessing capability. They are assessing risk — the probability that the promoted person will fail visibly, create problems, or reflect poorly on the decision-maker who championed them. Professionals who appear stable, composed, and organizationally fluent represent lower perceived risk. Those who appear frustrated, politically naive, or relationally difficult represent higher risk, regardless of their actual capability.

Composure. Political fluency. Credibility infrastructure. These are not separate from advancement strategy. They are advancement strategy.

The Sponsorship Gap

Under competent leadership, your direct manager serves as your sponsor, advocating for your advancement in discussions you are not part of. Under incompetent leadership, this channel degrades or fails.

The Conflict Avoider will not advocate forcefully for your promotion because advocacy requires confrontation with competing candidates and limited resources. The Credit Absorber has been presenting your work as their own, making it difficult to advocate for your advancement without undermining their narrative. The Absent Authority may not be present for the conversation at all. The Political Appointee will advocate for you only to the extent that your advancement serves their own positioning.

The result is a sponsorship gap: the absence of effective advocacy in the conversations that determine your trajectory.

Strategic Operators close this gap by building alternative sponsorship channels. The distributed credibility, political fluency, and translation capability built across earlier chapters converge here: each provides a channel for building sponsorship independent of your direct manager.

This does not require asking people to sponsor you. Direct requests for sponsorship are uncomfortable and typically counterproductive. Organic sponsorship emerges when the people who observe your work form genuine convictions about your readiness, and carry those convictions into rooms where decisions are made.

Elena has begun this work. Her skip-level relationships, built through cross-functional project visibility and genuine professional engagement, have created independent impressions of her capability with leaders above David. When a senior director mentioned in passing that Elena's project management on a recent initiative was "the best-run process in the division," Elena recognized that moment for what it was: distributed credibility producing organic sponsorship.

"David would never have said that about me — not because he disagrees, but because he doesn't think in those terms," Elena observes. "He would have said the project went well. He wouldn't have attributed it specifically. That attribution came from someone who observed my work directly, without David's filter."

That single observation, made in a room Elena was not in, may carry more weight than anything David has communicated about her in two years of performance reviews.

The Architecture of Leverage

Visibility creates awareness. Leverage creates options.

Five sources of professional leverage produce negotiating power, trajectory influence, and strategic choice independent of any single organizational relationship.

Expertise scarcity is leverage through irreplaceability. When you possess knowledge, skills, or capabilities that the organization cannot easily source elsewhere, your position strengthens. This does not require being the only person who can do what you do. It requires being difficult to replace without meaningful cost: in time, quality, institutional knowledge, or relationship continuity. The organizational expert on a critical system, the holder of key client relationships, the possessor of specialized knowledge that would take months to rebuild; each has leverage whether or not they ever invoke it.

Relationship capital is leverage through connection. The professional who has built genuine, reciprocal relationships across the organization (with decision-makers, influencers, peers, and external contacts) has an asset that cannot be replicated by hiring a replacement. Relationships are non-transferable. The trust, credibility, and goodwill you have built exist only in the context of you. This is leverage, even when it is never framed that way.

Operational criticality is leverage through embeddedness. When you are woven into processes, projects, or systems that the organization depends on, your departure creates disruption that decision-makers will prefer to avoid. This leverage increases over time as your operational footprint expands, but it also carries risk if it creates resentment rather than appreciation. The goal is to be valued for your contribution, not feared for the disruption your absence would create.

External options are leverage through alternatives. The professional who is valued by the external market, who receives recruiter inquiries, has a visible professional reputation, or maintains a network that generates opportunities, has options that provide both strategic alternatives and implicit negotiating power. You need not threaten to leave. The knowledge that you could leave, and that the organization would lose something meaningful, changes the dynamic.

Reputation capital is leverage through perception. The Credibility Compound, built systematically across your career, creates a cumulative reputation that opens doors, attracts opportunities, and positions you as someone worth investing in. This is the compound deployed for advancement: the same principle, now applied to trajectory rather than protection.

Marcus Chen has built all five sources of leverage, though he rarely thinks of them in those terms. His operational knowledge of the division is irreplaceable in the near term. His relationships with the CFO, with key clients, and with his cross-functional peers are assets the organization cannot transfer. His operational involvement in critical systems makes his departure costly. His external reputation generates periodic recruiter interest. And his credibility compound, built over fourteen years through consistent reliability, positions him as a leader worth retaining and advancing.

"I don't think of it as leverage," Marcus reflects. "I think of it as having options. The equity keeps me here for now. But knowing I could leave — and that the organization knows I could leave — means I negotiate from a different position than someone who has no alternatives."

Leverage means operating from strength. The professional who has it makes decisions from choice. The professional without it makes decisions from constraint.

Engineering Promotion Readiness

Leverage creates options. Promotion readiness creates the conditions where those options translate into advancement.

Many professionals deserve advancement and do not receive it. Readiness is the convergence of factors that make promotion likely: capability that is demonstrated, visibility that is established, sponsorship that is active, timing that is favorable, and risk perception that is low.

Strategic Operators engineer this convergence rather than waiting for it to occur naturally.

Signal capability at the next level. Decision-makers promote professionals who are already operating at the next level, not those who might be able to if given the opportunity. This means seeking work that demonstrates next-level capability before the title exists: leading initiatives that cross functional boundaries, making decisions that affect scope beyond your current role, demonstrating judgment that reflects broader organizational awareness. The promotion then ratifies what is already visible rather than gambling on potential.

Make your readiness legible. Decision-makers cannot promote what they cannot articulate. If your readiness requires explanation, if someone has to argue that your contributions are more significant than they appear, the promotion faces unnecessary friction. Strategic Operators ensure that their contributions are framed in terms that map directly to the criteria decision-makers use. When the organization values revenue impact, contributions framed in revenue terms register. When it values leadership capability, visible and documented leadership behaviors carry weight.

Build the advocacy network before the decision window. Sponsorship cannot be manufactured in the week before a promotion cycle. The relationships, impressions, and advocacy positions that determine the outcome were built over months. The professional who begins positioning three months before a promotion cycle is late. The professional who has been building distributed credibility and political capital continuously is ready whenever the cycle arrives.

Reduce perceived risk. Every promotion signal developed here (composure, political fluency, organizational awareness, relationship quality) reduces the perceived risk of advancing you. Decision-makers who feel confident that you will succeed at the next level, that you will not create problems, and that their advocacy will be validated by your performance are more likely to spend their own capital supporting your advancement.

In practice, visibility engineering is quiet.

After a successful cross-functional initiative (one that required Elena to coordinate delivery across three teams and recover a timeline that had slipped) she sends a brief update to her skip-level VP. The email is not about Elena. It is about the project.

"Hi Janet — wanted to flag that the Atlas integration is back on track for the March deadline. The delivery teams realigned on sequencing last week, and the vendor dependency that was creating the delay has been resolved through a revised SOW. Happy to provide more detail if useful for the Q1 review."

Three sentences. No self-attribution. No list of what Elena personally did. But the email establishes three things: Elena has direct knowledge of a high-priority initiative, the problems were solved, and Elena is the person providing this update — not David, not another director, but Elena.

The VP responds: "Thanks, Elena. Good to hear. Let's discuss in the Q1 prep meeting." Elena is now on the agenda for a meeting she would not otherwise attend.

A brief, useful communication that places the professional in the line of sight of a decision-maker while providing genuine value. The visibility is a byproduct of being useful — but the decision to send the email, to this person, at this moment, was strategic.

A senior analyst in a financial services firm wants to advance to a management role. Her direct manager, a classic Peter Principle Promotion, cannot articulate what management readiness looks like because he struggles with management himself. Rather than waiting for his sponsorship, she identifies two directors who have observed her work on cross-functional projects. She volunteers to lead a workstream that requires coordinating across three teams, management work in everything but title. When the promotion cycle arrives, her cross-functional leadership is documented, her relationships with decision-influencers are established, and two directors independently recommend her. Her manager's vague endorsement is supplemented by specific, credible advocacy from leaders who observed her operating at the next level.

The Visibility Trap Revisited

Performance alone does not produce advancement. That reality has a cost.

It costs time: time spent on relationship-building, visibility engineering, and strategic positioning that could otherwise be spent on the work itself. It costs cognitive load: persistent awareness of perception, reputation, and organizational dynamics. And it costs something harder to name: operating in a system that does not reward contribution as purely as it claims to.

Strategic Operators absorb this cost because the alternative is worse: stalled trajectory, passed-over opportunities, and the quiet erosion that follows excellent work no one who decides ever sees.

Elena recognizes this now in a way she did not at the beginning of her journey. The first time she was passed over, she experienced it as injustice. The second time, she experienced it as a pattern. Now she experiences it as a system she understands and is actively navigating.

"I still wish the work were enough," Elena admits. "But wishing doesn't produce promotions. Understanding the system does. And honestly, once I stopped resenting the system and started operating within it, the work got easier too. I'm not carrying the weight of feeling unseen anymore. I'm building the channels that make sure I'm seen."

Visibility is not vanity. It is the infrastructure that connects performance to trajectory, and without it, performance exists in isolation.

From Visibility to Movement

Options without activation are theoretical. What remains is the decision: when to move, how to move, and how to ensure that movement builds rather than discards.

Visibility is built. Leverage exists. What remains is deployment.

Chapter 11: Strategic Movement

Exits, Transitions, and Trajectory Engineering

The most common strategic error among competent professionals navigating dysfunction is not leaving too early. It is staying too long.

The infrastructure holds. The tools work. The professional who has built what these chapters describe is no longer powerless, no longer invisible, no longer at the mercy of one unreliable leader. Staying feels like the strategic choice — and for a time, it is.

But every situation has a strategic lifespan: a window during which it serves your trajectory and beyond which it begins to erode it. Recognizing where you are in that window is the final dimension of career engineering.

The Cost of Staying Too Long

The reasons are understandable. You have built infrastructure: relationships, credibility, documentation systems, political capital. Leaving means starting over, at least partially. The current situation is known; the next one is uncertain. There is always a reason to wait. A project to finish, a vesting milestone to reach, a reorganization that might improve things.

And so the professional stays. Another quarter. Another year. Another cycle of promising themselves they will move when conditions change.

The cost of this delay is not always visible in the moment. It accumulates gradually: in stalled development, in opportunities that pass while you wait, in the slow normalization of dysfunction that makes it harder to recognize what you are tolerating. The professional energy budget absorbs the damage quietly; compensation work expands, investment work contracts, and the deficit compounds quarter by quarter. The professional who stays three years under leadership that caps their growth may not notice the cost in any single quarter.

They notice it when they finally enter the market and discover that their peers, who moved strategically, are two levels ahead.

The question is not whether to leave. It is whether staying still serves your trajectory, or has become inertia dressed as strategy.

The Navigability Threshold

These tools dramatically expand what is navigable. They do not make everything navigable.

A situation is navigable when the dysfunction can be managed through the Strategic Operator's tools, when career trajectory continues to advance, even if imperfectly, and when the cost of staying does not exceed the value of remaining. Under navigable dysfunction, the professional is learning, building, positioning, and progressing. The situation is imperfect but workable.

A situation becomes non-navigable when the dysfunction overwhelms the tools available. Translation produces no movement. Documentation records a pattern of deterioration. Escalation has failed or is structurally impossible. The professional's development has stalled. Their health, relationships, or professional reputation are sustaining damage that infrastructure cannot offset.

The line between navigable and non-navigable is not always sharp. It often reveals itself through accumulation: the gradual recognition that the situation is no longer serving development, that the compensation costs are climbing, that the trajectory has flattened despite everything the professional is doing.

Strategic Operators track this threshold actively. They do not wait for a crisis to reveal that they should have moved six months ago.

The Strategic Exit Framework

The decision to move, whether internally or externally, benefits from the same structured evaluation that governs escalation.

The decision to move evaluates five dimensions.

Trajectory assessment. Is your career advancing in this situation? Not just in title or compensation, but in capability, reputation, and positioning for the next stage. If you are developing new skills, building valuable relationships, and accumulating credibility that will transfer, staying has trajectory value, even if the leadership is poor. If your development has plateaued and your capabilities are depreciating rather than compounding, the situation is costing you more than the dysfunction itself.

Timing analysis. Career moves exist within multiple timing contexts: the completion of a significant project that provides a strong narrative anchor; the organizational cycle (budget seasons, reorganizations, leadership transitions that create openings); and the external market (economic conditions, industry demand for your skills, the availability of roles that represent genuine advancement). Optimal timing aligns as many of these contexts as possible. Perfect timing rarely exists. But informed timing consistently outperforms reactive timing.

Direction evaluation. Internal transfers and external moves carry different risk profiles and require different preparation. Internal moves preserve organizational relationships, institutional knowledge, and accumulated political capital. They also carry the risk that your reputation from the current role, shaped by dysfunctional leadership, follows you. External moves offer a clean start but require rebuilding context, relationships, and credibility from the ground up. The right direction depends on whether the dysfunction is local (your leader, your division) or systemic (the organization's culture, incentive structures, leadership quality at scale).

Narrative positioning. How a departure is perceived matters for both the current and next position. The professional who leaves because they "couldn't handle" a difficult situation carries a different narrative than the one who moves to "pursue a strategic opportunity." The framing is not dishonest; Strategic Operators do not fabricate reasons. But they ensure that the true reason, strategic advancement, is the visible reason. Leaving should look like what it is: a deliberate career decision, not an escape.

Relationship preservation. The professional network built during a difficult situation is an asset that survives the departure, if managed well. Colleagues, cross-functional partners, skip-level leaders, and even the dysfunctional leader themselves may be valuable contacts in future contexts. Departures that burn bridges destroy assets that took years to build. Strategic exits maintain relationships through professional communication, appropriate notice, thorough hand-offs, and genuine appreciation for what was valuable in the experience.

Internal Transfers: Movement Within

For professionals whose dysfunction is local, limited to their direct leader or immediate team, internal transfer offers a powerful option. The organizational infrastructure remains. The accumulated credibility, relationships, and institutional knowledge transfer with you. The career continues without the disruption of a full organizational change.

Elena Vasquez has been building toward this move for months, though she would not have recognized it as such when she began.

Her distributed credibility (the lateral relationships, the skip-level visibility, the cross-functional project leadership) was initially built as protection against single-channel vulnerability. But it has produced something beyond protection: it has created demand. Two different directors in adjacent functions have observed her work directly. One has mentioned to her, informally, that he would welcome her on his team if she were ever interested.

Elena is interested. But she is also strategic.

"Six months ago, I would have jumped at that conversation," Elena reflects. "I was so frustrated with David that any exit would have felt like progress. Now I'm evaluating it differently. The role would need to advance my trajectory, not just remove me from a bad situation. Moving laterally to escape dysfunction is not the same as moving strategically to build capability."

The evaluation she conducts reflects the Strategic Exit Framework: the role offers new scope that develops leadership skills David's team cannot provide. The timing aligns with the completion of her current major project, giving her a strong narrative. The director who extended the informal invitation has a reputation for developing his team, a direct contrast to David. The move is lateral in title but developmental in substance. Her organizational political map confirms it: the director has genuine influence in the promotion discussions that matter, and the move repositions her favorably within the power structure she has spent months mapping.

Elena does not rush. She completes her project. She ensures her documentation is current and her handoff will be clean. She communicates to David with professional respect. She has learned more from navigating David's dysfunction than she expected. She does not need to say that to David. She says it to herself.

External Moves: Movement Beyond

When the dysfunction is systemic, when the organizational culture, incentive structures, or leadership quality at scale make internal movement insufficient, external exit becomes the strategic choice.

External moves carry higher disruption and higher potential return. The professional leaves behind accumulated political capital, institutional knowledge, and relationship proximity. They gain a clean slate, new development opportunities, and — if the move is well-timed — a meaningful advancement in scope, compensation, or trajectory.

Marcus Chen thinks about external movement more often than his composed exterior would suggest.

"I run two calculations in parallel," Marcus explains. "One is the internal calculation — equity vesting, operational leverage, the political landscape. That calculation currently favors staying. The other is the external calculation — what the market values about my experience, what roles exist that would represent genuine advancement, what my network can access. I keep that calculation current even when I don't intend to act on it."

The leverage architecture he has built (expertise, relationships, operational embeddedness, external options, reputation capital) gives both calculations their weight. Marcus is not preparing to leave. He is maintaining the optionality to leave, which is different. The professional who never evaluates external options loses awareness of their market value, lets their network atrophy, and faces a longer ramp-up when circumstances eventually force a move. The professional who maintains external awareness can move quickly when conditions change, negotiate from information rather than desperation, and ensure that staying is an active choice rather than passive default.

Marcus's equity vesting timeline, now approaching, is the most significant variable in his calculation. When the equity vests, the cost-benefit ratio of staying under James shifts substantially. The golden handcuffs open. What Marcus does next will depend on what the internal and external calculations say at that moment.

"I will not make that decision emotionally," Marcus states. "I will make it strategically, with full information, at the right time. I've earned that much."

Timing the Transition

The difference between a well-timed move and a poorly-timed one is often the difference between advancement and lateral displacement.

Complete before you depart. The professional who leaves mid-project leaves an impression of abandonment. The one who delivers a major outcome and then transitions leaves an impression of someone who finishes what they start and is ready for the next challenge. Whenever possible, time departures to follow significant completions.

Align with organizational cycles. Reorganizations create openings that don't exist during stable periods. Leadership transitions reset political dynamics.

Budget cycles determine when new positions are funded. The professional who understands these cycles can time internal moves to coincide with structural opportunity.

Read the external market. Industry hiring patterns, economic conditions, and demand for specific capabilities fluctuate. The professional who maintains external awareness, through recruiter relationships, industry networking, and market monitoring, can time external moves to coincide with strong demand for their skills.

Avoid reactive timing. The worst time to make a career move is immediately after a frustrating incident. The second worst is during a period of burnout when judgment is compromised. Strategic moves are made from positions of strength, not moments of weakness. The professional who has built sustainable operating patterns and maintains emotional regulation makes timing decisions from strategy, not desperation.

A marketing director has decided to leave her organization after two years under an Absent Authority who provides no strategic direction. She identifies three timing factors: her current campaign launches in six weeks and will produce measurable results; a competitor has posted a VP-level role that matches her experience; and the annual performance review cycle (during which her contributions will be formally documented) occurs in eight weeks. She waits. The campaign launches successfully. Her performance review captures the outcomes. She applies for the external role with fresh, documented evidence of impact. She receives the offer and gives notice three days after her review is finalized. The timing converts what could have been a frustrated departure into a strategic advancement.

The Narrative of Departure

How you leave shapes how you are remembered, and how you are remembered shapes what comes next.

The professional who departs with visible frustration, who criticizes leadership on the way out, who fails to manage the narrative of their exit, damages the very network they spent years building. Exit interviews that become grievance sessions may feel cathartic. They are rarely strategic.

The Strategic Operator controls the narrative. The departure is framed as opportunity-driven: a new challenge, a growth opportunity, a strategic next step. The move is strategic. The opportunity is real. The fact that dysfunction also motivated the move is true but not useful to broadcast.

Calibrate what information serves your interests and what does not. Specific, documented feedback about organizational dynamics, delivered professionally and constructively, can be appropriate. Emotional venting about a specific leader is rarely valuable and frequently damaging.

Every departure is also a beginning. The impression you leave is the first signal your former colleagues will transmit about you in the conversations that follow.

Forced Moves and Strategic Recovery

Not all career moves are chosen. Layoffs, reorganizations, and organizational failures create forced transitions that the professional did not initiate and may not have wanted.

The Strategic Operator's response to a forced move is the same framework applied to a chosen one (assessment, timing, direction, narrative, relationships) compressed into shorter timelines under greater pressure.

The critical difference is narrative. A forced departure carries stigma in some professional contexts, even when the cause was entirely organizational. The professional who was laid off during a restructuring may face skepticism from future employers about whether the restructuring was the real reason.

Strategic Operators manage this by controlling what they can: their own story. The narrative of a forced move should be factual, professional, and forward-oriented. What happened, briefly. What you learned. What you're looking for. The emphasis is on trajectory, not grievance.

Your documentation infrastructure serves a critical function here. The professional who has maintained an evidence base of contributions, outcomes, and professional value can reconstruct their narrative quickly and credibly, without depending on a former organization's willingness to provide it.

The Movement Mindset

The movement mindset treats every position as a chapter, not the entire story. It evaluates each role against trajectory: what is being built, what is being learned, what is being positioned for. It maintains readiness to move even when the current situation is satisfactory, because conditions change and preparation cannot be manufactured retroactively.

This is not restlessness. The professional who is always ready to move is not always moving. They are simply never trapped.

The deepest question remains: not how to navigate dysfunction, not how to position for advancement, but who you become through the process. What you extract from this adversity determines whether you become a leader who builds what was never built for you — or one who perpetuates the patterns you endured.

What remains is the final transformation: converting everything this adversity has taught into the leadership that ensures you never create what you have navigated.

PART V: EVOLVE INTO LEADERSHIP

Chapter 12: The Counter-Curriculum

What Broken Leadership Teaches Those Who Pay Attention

Every professional who has navigated incompetent leadership can inventory the costs with precision. The time. The energy. The opportunities that dysfunction consumed. The professional development that should have happened under competent guidance and did not. They carry these costs.

Fewer can articulate what the experience taught them.

Cost is the visible product of adversity. Curriculum is the hidden one. The frustration, the wasted effort, the leadership failures observed at close range — these register as damage. They are also data. And the professional who learns to extract that data deliberately acquires a leadership education that no program and no case study can replicate.

The question is developmental: What did that teach me? And what kind of leader does it equip me to become?

Enduring vs. Studying

Most professionals who survive leadership dysfunction endure it. They cope, adapt, compensate, and eventually move on. They carry the experience as a scar: something that happened to them, something they are relieved to have behind them, something they prefer not to think about too carefully.

A smaller number of professionals do something different. They study it.

Enduring and studying are not mutually exclusive. The professional who studies dysfunction while navigating it is not above the frustration. They feel every cost. They simply also observe, with diagnostic precision, what is happening and why.

The professional who can name a Conflict Avoider, who can describe the specific mechanism by which conflict avoidance distributes cost to the team, who can articulate why the behavior persists despite its consequences — that professional has not merely survived a difficult situation. They have acquired knowledge about leadership that most programs attempt to teach and few deliver with this clarity.

Because the knowledge is experiential. It is not abstract. Leadership development studies bear this out: roughly 70% of leadership capability develops from challenging on-the-job experiences. Working under a bad boss is explicitly identified as one of the most productive developmental categories. Formal coursework accounts for about 10%. The curriculum no one would choose turns out to be the one that teaches the most. The professional who has spent two years translating for a leader who cannot receive direct communication understands something about organizational communication that no case study can replicate. The professional who has watched a Credit Absorber systematically erode team trust understands something about attribution and morale that no leadership seminar captures with the same specificity. The professional who has maintained their own composure while a Political Appointee made commitments they could not fulfill understands something about the relationship between competence and authority that theoretical models only approximate.

But this knowledge is only valuable if extracted deliberately. Left unprocessed, it produces cynicism or simple relief at having escaped. Processed with intention, it produces something rarer: a leadership education built on direct observation of failure.

The Lessons Dysfunction Carries

Every leadership failure teaches something specific. Not a vague lesson about "what not to do," but a precise understanding of a mechanism that doesn't work, a behavior that costs more than it produces, a gap between what a leader intends and what their actions actually generate.

The Conflict Avoider teaches the cost of unresolved tension. The professional who has worked under a conflict-avoidant leader has watched decisions unmade, conversations unfinished, and problems compounding beneath a surface of artificial calm. They have seen the downstream effects: the team members who fill the leadership vacuum with their own competing directions, the stakeholders who lose trust in a function that cannot commit, the talented professionals who leave because their development requires feedback their manager will never deliver. The lesson is not simply that avoidance is bad. It is a detailed understanding of the mechanism: how avoidance propagates, what it costs at each stage, and why leaders engage in it despite the cost.

The Credit Absorber teaches what attribution really means. The professional who has watched their contributions absorbed into someone else's narrative understands, viscerally, how recognition shapes motivation, retention, and trust. They have experienced what it feels like to deliver excellent work and receive no signal that it was seen. They understand that attribution is not a courtesy. It is an infrastructure of trust, and when it fails, the damage extends far beyond one person's morale.

The Political Appointee teaches the gap between authority and capability. The professional who has reported to a leader placed for political reasons rather than functional expertise has observed what happens when decisions are made without operational understanding: the commitments that cannot be fulfilled, the strategies that ignore implementation reality, the gap between what leadership announces and what the organization can actually deliver.

The Micromanager Without Expertise teaches what trust enables. The professional who has been micromanaged by someone who does not understand the work they are managing has experienced the inverse of trust: the constant friction of review without insight, oversight without value, control without comprehension. They understand that autonomy is not permission to be unsupervised. It is the organizational recognition that the professional closest to the work is best positioned to execute it.

The Absent Authority teaches what presence means. Not physical presence — leadership presence. The professional who has operated under a leader who is nominally in charge but functionally absent understands what teams actually need from leadership: direction, prioritization, obstacle removal, and the willingness to make decisions that only the leader's position can make. They understand that leadership is not an identity. It is a set of functions that someone must perform, and when no one performs them, the team absorbs the cost.

Each archetype carries a curriculum. The question is whether the professional extracts it or merely escapes it.

The Counter-Example Curriculum

Extracting curriculum from dysfunction is not automatic. Without structure, the lessons remain diffuse — grievances rather than usable knowledge.

The process operates in four stages.

Specificity. Name the exact behavior you observed — the specific action or inaction and its specific consequences. "My manager was bad at communication" is a grievance. "My manager avoided delivering critical feedback, which resulted in team members repeating preventable errors for months because they didn't know their approach was flawed" is a lesson. The professional who can describe the mechanism with precision has learned something transferable.

Mechanism. Understand why the behavior fails. What does it cost, and to whom? What organizational dynamic does it create? Why does the leader engage in it despite the cost? What function does the dysfunction serve for the leader themselves? This analysis converts surface observation into structural understanding. The Conflict Avoider avoids conflict not because they fail to see it, but because the short-term discomfort of confrontation outweighs, in their personal calculus, the distributed long-term cost of avoidance. Understanding this mechanism does not excuse the behavior. It illuminates it — and that illumination is precisely what prevents the observer from replicating it. You do not avoid a trap you can see.

Inversion. Define the effective alternative with the same specificity you applied to the dysfunction. If the failure was avoiding critical feedback, the inversion is not simply "give feedback." It is: deliver specific, timely, behaviorally grounded feedback in a private setting, with clarity about the impact of the behavior and the change expected, delivered with enough professional respect that the recipient can act on it without defensiveness. The inversion must be as detailed as the observation. Vague commitments to "be better" produce vague results. Specific counter-patterns produce practiced capability.

Integration. Practice the counter-pattern in your current role, not someday when you have formal authority, but now, in whatever scope you currently occupy. The professional who leads a project team can practice the feedback discipline they wished their manager had. The professional who mentors a junior colleague can practice the attribution they never received. The professional who facilitates a cross-functional meeting can practice the decisiveness they watched their Conflict Avoider fail to exercise. Leadership capability is developed through practice, not promotion. The counter-curriculum is only curriculum if it is applied.

The professional who has completed this process for even three or four specific behaviors has a leadership education that is, in certain dimensions, superior to what most formal programs provide — grounded in direct observation, emotional salience, and the kind of detail that only sustained exposure produces.

What Elena Learned

Elena Vasquez is three months into her new role.

The transfer she engineered, from David's team to a director whose reputation for developing people was part of what drew her, has confirmed what she hoped. Her new leader provides clear direction, delivers feedback directly, and makes decisions without the endless deferral that characterized David's management. The contrast is immediate and, at times, disorienting.

"The first time my new director told me something I'd done wasn't working, I almost didn't know how to respond," Elena admits. "Not because the feedback was harsh — it wasn't. Because I'd gone so long without receiving any direct feedback at all. David would have let me keep doing it wrong for six months rather than have that conversation."

The disorientation fades. The curriculum does not.

Elena has begun cataloging what David taught her. Not what he intended to teach, which was nothing, but what his dysfunction revealed about the behaviors she will practice and the behaviors she will not.

"David taught me that avoiding conflict doesn't make it disappear. It just changes who bears the cost," Elena says. "Every time David declined to address a performance issue, the rest of the team absorbed the impact. Every time he smoothed over a disagreement instead of resolving it, the disagreement went underground and resurfaced worse. I watched this happen dozens of times. I could draw you the exact pattern."

She can. And that pattern, observed with the diagnostic precision she has cultivated, has become a specific commitment. When Elena leads a team of her own, she will not avoid difficult conversations. Not because she has read that feedback is important. Because she has experienced, in granular detail, what its absence produces.

But there is a subtler lesson, one that surprises her.

"David also taught me something about patience that I didn't expect," Elena reflects. "Not his patience — mine. Learning to translate for him, to present information in ways he could receive, to work within his limitations rather than just resenting them — that developed a capability I didn't have before. I'm more adaptable now. I understand that communication is not just about being right. It's about being received. I wouldn't have learned that under a competent leader, because a competent leader would have met me where I was."

Dysfunction does not only teach by negative example. Sometimes it develops capabilities that comfort would not have required. The professional who has learned to translate for a difficult leader has a communication skill that the professional who has only worked under receptive leaders may never develop.

What Marcus Built

Marcus Chen's counter-curriculum has been operating for years, though he has never called it that.

Fourteen years across multiple organizations, under leaders ranging from a Credit Absorber who claimed his strategic analysis as her own to James, whose political appointment left the entire division navigating the gap between authority and comprehension, Marcus has accumulated a body of observation that shapes his leadership of forty people every day.

"I run my team as a direct response to what I've observed," Marcus says. "Not consciously, most of the time. But when I trace back why I do certain things — why I insist on specific attribution in every presentation, why I hold one-on-ones weekly without exception, why I never commit my team to a timeline without consulting the people who will execute it — the answer is usually that I watched someone do the opposite and saw what it cost."

The attribution practice comes from the Credit Absorber. Marcus observed, early in his career, how systematically claiming others' work destroyed not just morale but the quality of information that flowed upward. Team members who knew their contributions would be absorbed stopped volunteering their best thinking. The leader got credit for diminishing returns. Marcus attributes specifically and publicly, not as generosity, but as an operational practice that sustains the flow of good ideas.

The one-on-one discipline comes from the Absent Authority pattern he has observed in colleagues' reporting lines. Leaders who cancel one-on-ones, who are perpetually unavailable, who manage by exception rather than by engagement. Marcus has watched the downstream effects. Team members drift. Priorities misalign. Problems that would have been caught in a fifteen-minute conversation become crises that consume weeks. His weekly one-on-ones are non-negotiable, and they are substantive: not status updates, but development conversations where he ensures he understands each person's work well enough to remove obstacles and provide direction.

The commitment discipline comes from James. Marcus has spent years watching a leader commit his division to deliverables conceived without operational understanding. He has rebuilt timelines, restructured workloads, and absorbed the consequences of promises his leader made without consulting the people who would fulfill them. His counter-pattern is absolute: no commitment is made on his team's behalf without the people doing the work validating the feasibility. This is not consensus-seeking. It is operational competence.

"James is the most expensive education I've ever received," Marcus observes. "The tuition was years of my career. But the curriculum was specific. I know exactly what happens when a leader doesn't understand the function they lead. I know what it costs the people below them. I know what it looks like from the inside. And I know, with precision, what I do differently because of it."

Marcus's leadership of his team is a running answer to the leadership failures he has observed.

The Cynicism Trap

The professional who studies dysfunction closely — who catalogs failures, analyzes mechanisms, and builds counter-models — operates near a gravitational field that can pull their analysis into something darker: generalized cynicism about leadership, organizations, and the possibility that competence and authority can coexist.

The cynical professional has seen too much dysfunction to believe in functional leadership. They enter new roles already expecting failure. They interpret every leadership decision through a lens of suspicion. They cannot receive competent leadership when it arrives because their diagnostic framework has become a filter that screens for dysfunction and discounts everything else.

This is the counter-curriculum corrupted — the same analytical capability that produces insight, turned toxic by overgeneralization.

The signs are recognizable. The professional who cannot name a leader they respect, not in their current organization, not in any organization, has crossed the line from diagnostic precision into diagnostic distortion. The professional who interprets every organizational decision as evidence of incompetence has lost the calibration that distinguishes genuine dysfunction from normal organizational complexity. The professional who finds satisfaction in identifying failure but no motivation to build alternatives has substituted analysis for action.

The antidote is specificity. Cynicism operates in generalities: leaders are incompetent, organizations are broken, the system is rigged. The counter-curriculum operates in particulars: this specific leader fails in this specific way, producing these specific consequences, which I will counter with these specific practices. Maintaining specificity is what keeps analysis from calcifying into ideology.

Elena has felt the pull. In her early months navigating David, the frustration was generalized, a diffuse anger at organizational dysfunction that colored her perception of the entire company. The diagnostic framework from Chapter 2 began to change that. Naming David's specific pattern, Conflict Avoider, separated his dysfunction from a general indictment of leadership. The more precisely she could describe what was failing, the less the failure felt universal.

"There was a period where I was becoming the person who complains about everything," Elena acknowledges. "Every leadership decision was wrong. Every manager was incompetent. I was turning into someone I didn't respect. The shift came when I started being specific. David has a specific problem. It produces specific costs. But my new director doesn't have that problem. My skip-level leader doesn't have it. The VP I worked with on the cross-functional project was genuinely excellent. Once I could see the specifics, I could see that dysfunction was real but not universal. That distinction matters."

The professional whose counter-curriculum has been corrupted into cynicism will eventually become a leader who trusts no one, delegates nothing, and creates the very conditions they once diagnosed in others.

Building Counter-Models

The counter-curriculum produces behavioral commitments. Counter-models go further; they produce a coherent picture of the leader you intend to become, assembled from the inverse of what you have observed.

A counter-model is not an ideal. It is specific and operational — built from the particular failures you witnessed, inverted with the same precision you used to diagnose them, and integrated into a leadership approach that is uniquely yours because it responds to the specific curriculum your career has provided.

No two professionals build the same counter-model, because no two professionals observe the same failures in the same sequence with the same salience. The professional who spent formative years under a Credit Absorber builds a counter-model that emphasizes attribution, trust, and the protection of team contributions. The professional who navigated a Micromanager Without Expertise builds a counter-model that emphasizes autonomy, trust in expertise, and the restraint to oversee without controlling. The professional who endured an Absent Authority builds a counter-model that emphasizes presence, decisiveness, and the active performance of the leadership functions that no one else can perform.

Generic commitments to "be a good leader" are well-intentioned and operationally empty. A commitment to "ensure that every team member's contribution is specifically attributed in every presentation to senior leadership, because I experienced what happens when it isn't" is a practice. Practices produce behavior, shape culture, and determine the organizational environment your team inhabits.

A product director spent four years reporting to a leader who never prioritized. Every initiative was equally urgent, every request was top priority, and the team existed in a state of perpetual overcommitment. The dysfunction was specific: the inability to say no, or even "not yet," to any stakeholder request. The product director observed the mechanism in detail: how the lack of prioritization created competing workstreams, how team morale degraded under impossible expectations, how the leader's unwillingness to make hard choices transferred those choices to individual contributors who lacked the context to make them well. When she eventually led her own product team, her counter-model was built around a single principle: the leader's primary function is to decide what the team will not do. Every sprint begins with her explicitly naming the requests being deferred and the reason for deferral. Her team consistently delivers. They describe her leadership as "the most focused environment they've worked in." She describes it as a direct response to four years of observing the cost of its absence.

The Curriculum Continues

The counter-curriculum is not a one-time exercise. It is an ongoing practice, a discipline of observation, analysis, and integration that continues as long as the professional is exposed to leadership, which is to say, for the duration of their career.

New situations produce new observations. The professional who moves into a new role encounters new leaders with new patterns. The professional who advances into management observes leadership dynamics from a different vantage point, seeing how organizational pressure shapes the very behaviors they once diagnosed from below. The professional who reaches senior levels discovers that some of the dysfunction they observed was not incompetence but constraint, the product of pressures and trade-offs that were invisible from their earlier position.

This discovery does not invalidate the counter-curriculum. It refines it. The mature leader understands that some of what looks like dysfunction from below is actually the imperfect management of competing demands, and some of what looks like competing demands from above is actually dysfunction dressed in strategic language. The ability to distinguish between the two is itself a product of diagnostic capability.

Marcus has reached this level of refinement. He no longer views every leadership failure as simple incompetence. Some of what James does (the political positioning, the stakeholder management, the careful calibration of what to communicate to the board) reflects legitimate leadership challenges that Marcus, from his position, initially dismissed.

"I still think James is wrong for this role," Marcus clarifies. "His gaps are real. But I've also come to understand that some of what I interpreted as pure political maneuvering is actually organizational navigation at a level I haven't operated at yet. The lesson isn't that James is competent. It's that organizational leadership at the SVP level involves complexities I need to understand before I operate there. Even bad leaders can teach you about the terrain they're failing to navigate."

Diagnostic maturity: the capacity to extract lessons not only from what a leader does wrong but from the system they are operating within when they do it.

The curriculum is extracted. What follows is its application: leadership exercised before the title arrives.

Chapter 13: Leading Before the Title

Authority-Free Leadership and Influence-Based Impact

Somewhere in every organization, a competent professional is waiting.

They have navigated dysfunction, built credibility, developed political fluency, and assembled a counter-curriculum of lessons about what leadership should look like. They know what they would do differently. They have opinions about direction, strategy, and how teams should be run.

They are waiting for the title.

The assumption is understandable. Leadership, as most organizations define it, is a positional concept: a set of responsibilities conferred through formal authority. You become a leader when you are promoted into a leadership role. Before that, you are an individual contributor, a team member, a professional who executes rather than directs. The title comes first. The leadership follows.

This assumption is backwards.

The professionals who succeed most consistently in leadership roles are not those who begin leading when the title arrives. They are those who have been leading — in practice, in influence, in the way they operate — long before anyone formally authorized them to do so. The title, when it comes, endorses what is already visible. The professional who waits for authority to begin leading faces a different outcome: they receive the title and discover that authority alone does not produce the capability, the followership, or the organizational influence that effective leadership requires.

The practice begins before the position exists: exercising influence, creating direction, building followership, and developing the leadership capability that formal authority can amplify but cannot create.

Authority-Based vs. Influence-Based Leadership

Authority-based leadership operates through formal power. The leader directs because they have the organizational right to direct, and team members comply because the reporting line requires compliance. Decisions are made and implemented through the hierarchical mechanisms the organization provides: performance reviews, resource allocation, task assignment, career influence.

Authority-based leadership is real. It exists, it functions, and when exercised competently it produces organized, effective teams. But it has a limitation that many leaders discover too late: compliance is not the same as commitment, and authority alone does not produce the trust, initiative, or creative investment that distinguishes functional teams from exceptional ones.

Influence-based leadership operates through a different mechanism entirely: clarity rather than directive, credibility rather than hierarchy, investment rather than obligation. The influence-based leader cannot evaluate performance, assign tasks, or affect compensation. What they have is less visible and more durable: the trust, respect, and professional confidence of people who follow because the leader has earned the right to be followed.

Every professional has encountered influence-based leaders, whether they recognized them as such. The senior individual contributor whose technical judgment shapes the team's direction. The project lead whose cross-functional coordination produces alignment that no org chart requires. The peer whose advice is sought because their perspective consistently clarifies complex problems. These professionals lead without authority. Their influence operates through competence, reliability, relationship, and the accumulated evidence that following their direction produces good outcomes.

The Strategic Operator has been building this infrastructure — often without recognizing it as leadership.

The Leadership You Already Practice

The infrastructure is already built.

Diagnostic capability that reads team dynamics before others have named the problem. Emotional regulation that provides stability others orient toward. Credibility through which influence flows across organizational boundaries. Translation capability that mobilizes diverse stakeholders around shared objectives. Political fluency that navigates the landscapes where leadership actually operates.

These are leadership capabilities. The Strategic Operator who has built them is already leading.

Four Dimensions of Influence-Based Leadership

Four dimensions of authority-free leadership define where the professional without formal power creates impact.

Direction through clarity. The most fundamental act of leadership is defining where work should go and why. In authority-based leadership, direction is communicated through directives: assignments, mandates, strategic plans issued from above. In influence-based leadership, direction is created through articulation: the ability to frame a problem clearly enough, define an objective compellingly enough, and map a path convincingly enough that others choose to follow it.

The professional who can walk into a meeting where five people have five different understandings of the problem and produce a shared understanding that focuses effort — that professional is leading. They have not been assigned the right to direct. They have earned it by being the person whose clarity resolves confusion.

Credibility through demonstrated competence. Influence-based leaders are followed because they are trusted, and trust, in professional contexts, begins with competence. The professional whose work is consistently excellent, whose judgment is consistently reliable, and whose commitments are consistently honored builds a form of authority that no title can replicate and no reorganization can remove.

The Credibility Compound, now operating as leadership asset. The professional who has built distributed credibility across the organization has built the foundation for influence-based leadership. People seek their input, defer to their expertise, and follow their direction not because they must, but because experience has demonstrated that doing so produces good outcomes.

Investment through development. The leader who invests in others' success builds followership that outlasts any project or reporting relationship. This investment takes many forms: the senior professional who mentors a junior colleague, sharing knowledge that accelerates their development. The project lead who ensures every contributor's work is visible and attributed. The peer who provides honest, specific feedback when the formal leader will not, because their counter-curriculum taught them what the absence of feedback costs.

Investment produces strategic benefit, but that is not why it matters. Leadership exists in the space between people — in the quality of attention, guidance, and support that one professional provides to another. The professional who has experienced the failure of this investment under dysfunctional leadership understands its value with a clarity that the professional who has always had competent mentorship may not.

Coordination through relationship. Organizations are not machines. They are networks of relationships, and work that crosses boundaries (functions, teams, divisions) flows through those relationships or does not flow at all. The professional who has built genuine, reciprocal relationships across the organization can coordinate efforts that their formal position would never authorize. They can align perspectives between teams that don't share a reporting line. They can resolve conflicts between functions that a manager in either function could not bridge. They can mobilize resources through trust and reciprocity rather than requisition and authority.

The professional whose network extends beyond their immediate team has influence that extends beyond their immediate team. That influence is leadership: informal, unrecognized by the org chart, and often more effective than the formal variety.

Elena Leading

Elena Vasquez does not think of herself as a leader. She is a Senior Program Manager, a role that carries coordination responsibility but not direct authority over the people she works with. She does not evaluate anyone's performance. She does not approve anyone's time off. She has no budget authority, no hiring authority, no formal power over any of the cross-functional team members whose work she helps organize.

She leads anyway.

"I didn't realize it until my new director pointed it out," Elena says. "He told me, three weeks into the role, that the cross-functional team was already looking to me for direction. Not because anyone told them to. Because I was providing clarity they weren't getting anywhere else."

The clarity Elena provides is a direct product of the capabilities she built navigating David. The diagnostic precision that allowed her to read David's conflict avoidance now allows her to read team dynamics, identifying where alignment is breaking down, where competing priorities are creating friction, where a decision is needed that no one has yet been willing to make. The translation capability that allowed her to frame information for David now allows her to frame objectives for diverse stakeholders: engineering and marketing and operations, each with different concerns, receiving the same strategy in terms that connect to their specific priorities.

The credibility she built through distributed reputation during her years under David has followed her. Cross-functional peers who worked with her on earlier projects trust her judgment. New colleagues observe the trust that existing relationships demonstrate and calibrate accordingly. Her credibility compound is producing returns in a new context, with new people. Reputation, once built, travels.

But the leadership behavior that Elena finds most meaningful is the one she learned from David's absence.

"I give feedback," Elena states. "Specifically, directly, and as close to the moment as I can. When a team member's approach isn't working, I tell them — respectfully, but clearly. When someone's contribution is excellent, I name it specifically and make sure it's visible. I do this because I spent two years receiving neither. I know what that absence costs. It's the one thing I can do now, without any title at all, that makes the most difference."

Her new director has noticed. Not because Elena reported it, but because the team's performance under her coordination has been measurably stronger than under the previous program manager. The director has begun giving her expanded scope: more complex projects, higher-stakes stakeholder relationships, work that develops her toward the management role she is now openly pursuing.

"I'm not waiting for the title anymore," Elena says. "I'm building the capability. The title will come when it comes. But the leadership is happening now."

Marcus Developing Leaders

Marcus Chen's relationship to authority-free leadership is different from Elena's. He has the title. He has the authority. He leads forty people through formal organizational power.

But Marcus understands something that many titled leaders do not: the most impactful leadership he exercises is not the authority-based kind.

"I can assign tasks and approve time off," Marcus observes. "Any manager can do that. What actually makes this department work is the leadership that happens without my involvement — the senior engineers who mentor junior ones without being asked, the project leads who coordinate across teams because they've built the relationships, the individual contributors who speak up in meetings with clarity that redirects the conversation. That's the leadership that scales. Mine doesn't."

Marcus has become deliberate about developing authority-free leaders on his team. His approach is shaped by the counter-curriculum, specifically by the inverse of what he observed under leaders who either hoarded leadership or failed to exercise it.

He creates opportunities for his team members to lead without titles. Project leads are given genuine autonomy, not the performative autonomy of a leader who delegates and then overrides, but the real autonomy of a leader who trusts the person closest to the work to make the decisions that proximity enables. When a project lead makes a call that Marcus might have made differently, he does not intervene unless the decision creates genuine risk. The trust is operational, not rhetorical.

He attributes with intention, the counter-curriculum practice now operating as leadership infrastructure, redirecting recognition to the specific contributors who produced it.

He provides the feedback his own leaders often didn't. Weekly one-on-ones are substantive: not task reviews, but development conversations. He tells his team members what they are doing well with specificity, what they could improve with equal specificity, and what he observes about their trajectory. Several of his senior team members have told him that his feedback is the most useful they have received in their careers. Marcus reads this as a data point about how rarely organizations develop this capability in their leaders.

"I'm trying to build people who won't need this book," Marcus says. "That's the real measure. Not whether my department hits its metrics — though it does. Whether the people who work here are developing the capability to operate strategically, lead effectively, and navigate whatever system they find themselves in. That's what I didn't get from the leaders above me. That's what I owe the people below me."

Leading Among Equals

The hardest form of authority-free leadership is leading peers.

Leading downward without authority (mentoring junior colleagues, guiding team members on a project) carries a natural asymmetry. Experience, expertise, and seniority create an informal hierarchy that makes influence feel organic. The junior colleague accepts guidance because the senior professional has credibility the junior colleague has not yet built.

Leading peers (professionals at the same level, with comparable experience, and without any hierarchical relationship) requires a different form of influence. There is no asymmetry to lean on. The peer who attempts to direct other peers through implicit authority they do not hold generates resentment, not followership. The peer who positions themselves above their colleagues, through tone, assumption, or behavior, damages relationships rather than building them.

Effective peer leadership operates through three mechanisms. First, facilitation rather than direction — the peer leader creates conditions for collective clarity: surfacing assumptions, organizing complex information, proposing structures that enable productive work. Their contribution is not the answer but the process by which the group arrives at one.

Second, competence without competition. The professional who consistently provides excellent analysis, useful perspective, and reliable follow-through earns influence among peers. The professional who provides those things while positioning themselves as superior loses it. The line is subtle but consistent: contribution builds peer influence; self-promotion erodes it.

Third, first-follower dynamics. Among peers, one of the most powerful acts of leadership is not proposing direction but supporting it: being the first to align behind a colleague's good idea, lending credibility to a proposal that needs momentum. The first follower often contributes more to movement than the initial proposer — influence exercised not through vision but through the judgment to recognize and amplify someone else's.

A senior data analyst in a consulting firm notices that three project teams are independently building similar data pipelines, duplicating effort because no coordination mechanism exists across the teams. She has no authority over any of the teams. She drafts a brief comparison of the three approaches, identifying where they overlap and where a shared component would eliminate redundancy. She sends it to the three team leads (peers, all of them) framed not as a directive but as an observation: "I noticed we're solving the same problem three times. Here's what I see. Would it be worth a conversation?" Two of the three leads engage. Within a month, a shared pipeline component exists, saving an estimated four hundred engineering hours over the quarter. The analyst received no formal recognition for the coordination. She received something more durable: a reputation among peers as someone who sees across boundaries and creates value through observation. That reputation is the infrastructure for her next act of influence-based leadership, and the next one after that.

The Reputation That Precedes the Title

Authority-free leadership produces a secondary effect that the professional exercising it may not immediately recognize: it builds the case for formal authority.

Decision-makers evaluating promotion candidates are assessing, among other factors, whether the candidate can lead: not whether they might be able to if given the opportunity, but whether they already do. The candidate who can point to influence exercised, direction created, followership earned, and coordination accomplished, all without formal authority, presents a fundamentally different profile than the candidate who promises they will learn to lead once the role is given.

Signal capability at the next level by demonstrating it at the current level. Not performance. Genuine leadership, exercised within whatever scope currently exists.

Elena's new director sees this. He does not see a program manager who might be ready for a management role. He sees a professional who is already leading, creating direction for cross-functional teams, providing feedback that develops team members, building coordination through relationships that her position alone would not sustain. The question for him is not whether Elena can lead. It is when the formal role catches up to the informal practice.

This convergence is not guaranteed. The professional who leads brilliantly but invisibly may wait indefinitely. The professional who leads and ensures that leadership is visible to the people who make decisions positions themselves for the advancement that confirms what they are already doing.

The Strategic Operator does both: they lead because it is the right way to operate, and they ensure that the leadership is seen because visibility is the infrastructure that connects practice to trajectory.

From Practice to Identity

The professional who exercises leadership before the title is not positioning themselves for advancement. They are becoming a leader: developing the specific capabilities, habits, and instincts that effective leadership requires, through the only method that works. Practice develops capability. Capability becomes identity.

Elena is not performing leadership. She is leading. The capability was forged in adversity, refined through the counter-curriculum, and deployed in her current role. When the title arrives, the transition will be seamless. The title will name what is already true.

Marcus has lived this for years. His formal authority over forty people is the least interesting thing about his leadership. The most interesting thing is the daily practice: the attribution, the development, the trust, the feedback. A department where people develop, contribute their best work, and build capabilities that will serve them long after they leave his team.

But the adversity that produced the counter-curriculum also produced exposure. And exposure, without vigilance, becomes transmission.

The patterns you endured are capable of becoming the patterns you transmit. What follows is the discipline of ensuring they do not.

Chapter 14: Breaking the Cycle

The Immunity Imperative

There is something this book has not yet said directly, though it has been present beneath the surface of every chapter since Part V began.

Exposure to dysfunction creates the risk of transmitting it.

The professional who has spent years navigating incompetent leadership, who has built the diagnostic frameworks, the emotional infrastructure, the strategic toolkit, the counter-curriculum, does not want to hear that they may carry the very patterns they endured. They have done the work. They have studied the dysfunction with precision. They have identified counter-patterns and committed to practicing them. Surely the awareness itself is protection enough.

It is not.

Understanding dysfunction intellectually does not prevent replicating it behaviorally. The mechanisms of internalization are deeper than conscious analysis, more persistent than good intentions, and more subtle than any diagnostic framework can easily detect in oneself. The professional who can identify a Conflict Avoider across a conference table may not recognize conflict avoidance in their own behavior, because when it is yours, it does not feel like avoidance. It feels like judgment. It feels like choosing the right moment. It feels like strategic patience.

How Dysfunction Is Internalized

The internalization of dysfunctional leadership patterns does not happen through conscious adoption. No professional observes a Credit Absorber claiming their work and decides to do the same. No one watches a Conflict Avoider defer every hard conversation and thinks, "That seems effective — I should try it."

Internalization happens through normalization.

The professional who spends two years under a leader who avoids conflict experiences two years of conflict avoidance as the ambient operating condition.

Disagreements are smoothed over. Difficult conversations are deferred. Tension is managed through indirect channels rather than direct address. This environment does not teach the professional that avoidance is good. It teaches something more insidious: it teaches them what "normal" feels like. What people observe others actually doing is a more powerful predictor of their own behavior than what they believe they should do. The professional knows avoidance is wrong. Two years of ambient modeling have taught them it is standard.

When that professional eventually leads, whether formally or informally, they carry that calibration with them. Their threshold for what constitutes a necessary confrontation has shifted. Their instinct for when to address tension directly has been recalibrated by years of operating in an environment where tension was never addressed directly. They do not choose avoidance. They default to it, because default is shaped by environment, and their environment was shaped by dysfunction.

The same mechanism operates across all archetypes. The professional who worked under a Micromanager Without Expertise may develop an exaggerated need for control, not because they admired the micromanagement, but because operating under constant scrutiny normalized a level of oversight that they now unconsciously replicate. The professional who reported to a Political Appointee may have learned that political positioning matters more than operational substance, and while they consciously reject this lesson, their behavior under pressure may reveal that they absorbed it more deeply than they knew.

The internalization is deepest where the exposure was longest, the dysfunction most pervasive, and the professional most formative. Early-career exposure, when professional norms are still being established, carries disproportionate weight. The professional whose first manager was a Credit Absorber may spend years unconsciously protecting their own contributions with a vigilance that, turned outward, manifests as reluctance to share credit with their own team.

None of this is inevitable. But all of it is possible. And the first step in prevention is examining the mechanism rather than assuming that awareness alone provides protection.

Understanding vs. Embodying

The counter-curriculum operates at the level of conscious analysis: identify the dysfunction, understand the mechanism, define the inversion, practice the counter-pattern. This process produces knowledge and intention — but not automatically behavior.

The gap between understanding and embodying is the gap between knowing what you should do and doing it, particularly under the conditions where internalized patterns are most likely to surface. Those conditions are specific and predictable.

Under stress. When pressure mounts, cognitive bandwidth narrows. The professional operating under deadline pressure, organizational crisis, or interpersonal conflict does not have the luxury of consulting their counter-curriculum in real time. They react from instinct, and instinct is shaped by experience. The experience of navigating dysfunction has shaped instincts that may not align with the leadership they consciously intend.

In ambiguity. When the situation is unclear and the right course of action is uncertain, the professional defaults to patterns that feel familiar. If the familiar pattern was set under dysfunctional leadership, the default may be dysfunctional, not because the professional lacks better options, but because the brain, seeking efficiency in uncertainty, reaches for what it has practiced most.

During fatigue. Self-monitoring requires energy. The professional who is exhausted, by workload, by organizational complexity, by the cumulative demands of leadership, has less capacity for the deliberate self-observation that catching internalized patterns requires. Fatigue does not create dysfunction. It removes the barriers that prevent absorbed patterns from surfacing.

When authority arrives. There is a particular irony in this: the moment when the professional receives formal authority — the promotion, the team, the title — is the moment when internalized patterns are most likely to manifest. Authority amplifies whatever leadership patterns the professional carries. Under the pressure and complexity of a new leadership role, with less bandwidth for self-monitoring and more scope for impact, the patterns set by years of observation emerge in behavior for the first time.

The professional who enters a leadership role believing that their counter-curriculum has made them immune is the professional most at risk. Confidence reduces vigilance. And vigilance is what prevents the patterns from operating unchecked.

Elena's Reckoning

Elena Vasquez does not expect what happens in her fourth month in the new role.

She is leading a cross-functional initiative, the kind of project she has managed successfully before, now with expanded scope under her new director. Three workstreams are running in parallel. Two of them are on track. The third is not. The workstream lead, a peer in a different function, has missed two milestones and is not communicating the reasons clearly.

Elena knows what needs to happen. A direct conversation. Specific questions about the delays. Clear expectations for recovery. This is exactly the kind of intervention she has committed to providing: the inverse of David's avoidance, the counter-curriculum in action.

She does not have the conversation.

She tells herself she is waiting for the right moment. She tells herself the workstream lead is dealing with resource constraints she should be sensitive to.

She tells herself that raising the issue now might create tension that complicates the initiative's broader dynamics.

She catches herself on the third day.

"I was doing it," Elena says. "I was doing exactly what David did. Rationalizing the delay. Finding reasons to wait. Telling myself I was being strategic when I was actually being avoidant. And the worst part was how natural it felt. It didn't feel like avoidance. It felt like good judgment. It felt like being considerate. That's what David's avoidance probably felt like to David."

The recognition stops her. She schedules the conversation for the next morning. She prepares specific observations: the missed milestones, the communication gap, the impact on the other workstreams. She delivers the feedback directly, professionally, with the same clarity she wished David had provided. The workstream lead receives it well. The recovery plan is in place within a week.

But the experience shakes Elena in a way she does not expect.

"I've been telling myself for months that I learned from David. That I would never avoid the hard conversations. And then, the first time it was genuinely uncomfortable — the first time avoidance would have been easier — I defaulted to it. Not because I chose it. Because it was the pattern I lived in for two years. That's internalization. It doesn't care about your counter-curriculum. It operates beneath your intentions."

Elena's counter-curriculum was intact. Her knowledge was precise. But the behavioral default, set by two years of operating in an avoidant environment, surfaced under exactly the conditions that surface defaults: ambiguity about the right moment, concern about relational dynamics, and the seductive rationalization that delay was judgment rather than avoidance.

Elena caught it. Her diagnostic precision allowed her to recognize the pattern in herself. Three days in, not three months. The correction was swift. But the lesson is indelible: awareness is necessary and insufficient. Self-monitoring must be active, continuous, and supported by external feedback.

The Leadership Pattern Audit

Catching internalized patterns requires more than intention. It requires a systematic practice of self-examination that operates with the same diagnostic precision the professional has applied to others.

The practice is a periodic, structured self-assessment designed to detect internalized dysfunction before it becomes embedded leadership behavior.

The Audit operates in four stages.

Exposure inventory. Catalog the specific dysfunctional patterns you were exposed to, not in general terms, but with the specificity the counter-curriculum demands. "I worked under a bad manager" is not an inventory. "I spent twenty-six months under a leader who systematically avoided conflict, deferred every difficult conversation, and left the team to manage the consequences of unresolved tension" is an inventory. The specificity matters because it defines the search parameters for the next stage. You cannot scan for patterns you have not precisely identified.

Transmission scan. Examine your own behavior with the same diagnostic precision you applied to the leaders you observed. The scan is most productive when focused on the conditions where defaults emerge: How do you behave under stress? What do you do when a conversation is going to be uncomfortable? When you face ambiguity, what pattern do you default to? When you are tired, what leadership behaviors degrade first? The answers to these questions reveal where internalized patterns may be operating: not where you lead at your best, but where you lead at your most automatic.

External validation. Self-assessment has a structural limitation: the patterns most deeply internalized are the patterns least visible to the person carrying them. The Conflict Avoider does not experience avoidance as avoidance. The professional who has absorbed a control pattern does not experience excessive oversight as excessive. External feedback (from trusted colleagues, from direct reports willing to provide honest input, from peers who observe your leadership in action) provides the data that self-assessment alone cannot.

This stage requires openness. The professional must create conditions where honest feedback about their leadership behavior is genuinely safe to deliver and genuinely received when offered. This is not a standard feedback request. "How am I doing?" produces polite generalities. The effective question is specific: "When I'm under pressure, do you notice me avoiding conversations I should be having?" or "Have you seen me take credit for work that should be attributed to someone else?" Specific questions produce specific answers. Specific answers reveal specific patterns.

Correction protocol. Where the Audit reveals transmission, where internalized patterns are operating in your leadership behavior, the correction is not willpower. Willpower fails under the same conditions that surface the patterns: stress, ambiguity, fatigue. The correction is structural.

Structural correction means changing the conditions rather than relying on moment-to-moment self-control. The professional who discovers a tendency toward avoidance creates a practice: every difficult conversation identified is scheduled within forty-eight hours, with a trusted colleague who will ask whether the conversation happened. The professional who discovers a control pattern builds autonomy into their management system: delegation with clear outcomes and no interim review unless the team member requests it. The professional who discovers an attribution gap institutes a public naming practice: every team presentation begins with specific acknowledgment of individual contributions.

Structure converts intention into behavior. Behavior, repeated, becomes pattern. New patterns, over time, replace the old ones, not through insight alone, but through the deliberate engineering of different defaults.

Marcus's Vigilance

Marcus Chen performs a version of the Leadership Pattern Audit every quarter, though he has never formalized it in these terms.

"I ask myself two questions," Marcus says. "What am I doing that looks like James? And what am I doing that looks like Renata?"

Renata. The name surfaces for the first time. She was the Credit Absorber from early in Marcus's career, the leader who presented his strategic analysis as her own, whose systematic appropriation of team contributions Marcus describes as his most formative leadership experience.

"Renata taught me what attribution means by never providing it," Marcus explains. "My counter-curriculum on attribution is strong. I attribute constantly, specifically, publicly. But the Audit isn't about whether I attribute well. It's about where the pattern might have leaked into something I don't see as clearly."

The leak Marcus has identified is subtler than outright credit-taking. It manifests as narrative control. Marcus, shaped by years of watching leaders control the story of his work, has developed a tendency to control the story of his team's work, not by claiming credit, but by shaping how their contributions are presented. He selects which accomplishments are highlighted. He frames the narrative for senior leadership. His team's work is well-attributed, but the framing is his.

"One of my senior engineers pointed it out," Marcus admits. "She said, 'You always give us credit, but you also always decide what the credit is for.' She was right. I was attributing, but I was also controlling the narrative — which is a softer version of what Renata did. She controlled attribution. I was controlling framing. The mechanism is different. The dynamic is related."

Marcus's correction was structural. He now asks each project lead to draft their own summary of their team's contributions before Marcus compiles the division update. Their framing enters the narrative alongside his. The change is small in practice and significant in principle. It distributes narrative authority, not just attribution.

The James pattern is different. Marcus scans for political positioning: the tendency to frame decisions in terms of organizational optics rather than operational substance. James does this constantly, and Marcus, after years of operating in that environment, sometimes catches himself evaluating options through a political lens before an operational one.

"I caught myself last month calculating how a resource allocation decision would look to the CFO before I calculated whether it was the right decision for the team," Marcus says. "That's James. That's the Political Appointee pattern — optics before operations. I made the right call in the end. But the sequence mattered. The fact that my first instinct was political, not operational, told me the pattern is in there."

He watches for a third pattern too: the cynicism trap — diagnostic precision hardening into generalized distrust.

The self-monitoring is diagnostic — the same analytical lens applied to others, now turned inward with the same precision and the same strategic intent. Marcus does not punish himself for the patterns he detects. He corrects them, structurally, and continues to scan.

"I'll be doing this for the rest of my career," Marcus acknowledges. "It doesn't end. The exposure doesn't expire. But the vigilance gets easier — not because the patterns fade, but because the Audit becomes routine. You build it into how you operate, the same way you build documentation or relationship maintenance. It's just another practice."

Building Feedback Infrastructure

The Leadership Pattern Audit's third stage, external validation, addresses the structural limitation that no amount of self-awareness can overcome: you cannot see yourself the way others experience you.

Building feedback infrastructure means creating durable channels through which honest observations about your leadership behavior can reach you. Not once, during a formal review cycle, but continuously, as a feature of how you operate.

Trusted observers. Identify two or three colleagues (peers, not direct reports) whose judgment you trust and whose willingness to be direct you have verified. Give them specific permission to flag patterns. Not vague permission ("Tell me if you see anything") but targeted permission ("I know I have a tendency to avoid hard conversations. If you see me deferring something I should address, tell me directly."). Specificity makes the feedback possible. Vague mandates produce vague silence.

Direct report signals. The people you lead experience your patterns most directly, but they are also the least likely to report them, because you hold organizational power over their careers. Creating conditions where direct reports feel safe providing upward feedback requires more than announcing an open-door policy. It requires demonstrated receptivity: visibly acting on feedback when it is provided, never penalizing the source, and consistently seeking input about your own behavior with the same specificity you use in the Audit.

Pattern journaling. A private, brief record of moments where you noticed yourself defaulting to an internalized pattern, or where you wonder, in retrospect, whether a decision was influenced by an absorbed pattern rather than genuine judgment. The record serves two functions: it maintains the vigilance the Audit requires, and it produces data that reveals trends invisible in any single incident. The professional who journals three instances of deferred conversations in a month has a data point that a single instance would not have revealed.

A newly promoted engineering manager, eighteen months into her first leadership role, notices that her team has become reluctant to bring her problems. She investigates and discovers that her response to problems (immediate, detailed, hands-on intervention) has taught her team that raising an issue means losing autonomy over the solution. The pattern is not malicious. It comes from three years under an Absent Authority who never helped with anything, leaving her to solve every problem alone. Her counter-model was to be present, involved, helpful. But the internalized pattern, the belief that problems require her immediate personal involvement, has calcified into a form of micromanagement that her conscious analysis never intended. She discovers this through a direct report who, during a one-on-one, says carefully: "I sometimes hesitate to raise issues because I know you'll take them over." The feedback is the data point that her self-assessment could not produce. She restructures her response: when a problem is raised, she now asks, "What support do you need from me?" rather than immediately providing her own solution. The structural change produces a behavioral change. Within two months, her team is raising issues earlier, with more ownership, and with better outcomes.

The Immunity You Build

The professional who has navigated dysfunction does not develop natural immunity, the kind that prevents infection entirely. They develop something more like acquired immunity: the ability to recognize and respond to the pattern before it produces full-blown transmission.

Acquired immunity is not passive. It requires ongoing maintenance: the Leadership Pattern Audit, the feedback infrastructure, the structural corrections that convert intentions into practices. It operates through vigilance, not through the comfortable belief that the danger has passed.

But acquired immunity is real. The professional who actively monitors for internalized patterns, who has built external feedback channels, who corrects structurally rather than through willpower alone, that professional is substantially less likely to transmit dysfunction than the one who has never examined the question. And they are far less likely to transmit it than the leader who was never exposed to dysfunction at all but also never developed the diagnostic capability to recognize it in themselves.

The final paradox of the counter-curriculum: the professional who has navigated dysfunction and processed it deliberately is, in some dimensions, better equipped to lead than the professional who has only experienced functional leadership. Not because dysfunction is desirable. Because the process of navigating it (the diagnosis, the analysis, the counter-modeling, the self-monitoring) develops a depth of leadership self-awareness that more conventional development paths do not require.

Elena has this awareness now. The moment of catching herself avoiding a difficult conversation — painful as it was — produced something valuable: proof that her self-monitoring works. She caught the pattern. She corrected it. She knows what to watch for. The immunity is not perfect. It is practiced.

Marcus has maintained this awareness for years. His quarterly Audit, his structural corrections, his willingness to receive specific feedback about his patterns: these are not signs of insecurity. They are the practices of a leader who understands that leadership quality is not a fixed attribute. It is a discipline that requires attention, honesty, and the recognition that the patterns you endured are always capable of surfacing in the leader you are becoming.

The cycle addressed. What remains is the longest view: where a career strategy becomes a professional legacy, and the Strategic Operator becomes not a phase but an identity.

Chapter 15: The Long Game

Career Arcs, Professional Legacy, and What Actually Matters

Step back. Not from the work. From the frame. For fourteen chapters, the lens has been close: a specific leader, a specific situation, specific tools for navigating specific dynamics. The questions have been immediate and operational. How do I diagnose this? How do I stabilize? How do I influence, position, evolve? The urgency was real. The tools were necessary. The professional navigating dysfunction needs them now, in the current quarter, under the current leader.

But the current quarter is not the career. The current leader is not the last leader. The situation that feels consuming today will, in five years, be a chapter you reference in conversation ("When I worked under a Conflict Avoider at that tech services company") with the compressed clarity that only distance provides. What felt like the defining challenge of your professional life becomes one arc among many. The frustration fades. The lessons remain.

The long view matters. Not because the immediate tools are unimportant; they are essential. But because the professional who operates only at the immediate level, who navigates each situation without reference to the larger arc, risks winning every battle and discovering, decades later, that the war was about something they never addressed.

The long game is about what compounds. What you build across a career that no single situation can give you and no single situation can take away. The capabilities, the relationships, the reputation, the leadership identity: these are the assets that accumulate, role after role, organization after organization, leader after leader. They are the professional legacy that outlasts every position you hold.

Career Arcs vs. Career Moments

The professional in the middle of a difficult situation experiences it as defining. The frustration is immediate. The costs are tangible. The possibility that this is temporary, that it is one segment of a much longer trajectory, is intellectually available but emotionally distant.

The human mind weights the immediate more heavily than the eventual. The quarterly review that dismissed your contributions hurts more, in the moment, than the career-long reputation that will render that single review irrelevant. The leader who is blocking your development feels more consequential, today, than the five or six future leaders who will have the opportunity to accelerate it.

Strategic Operators learn to hold both time horizons simultaneously: the immediate situation that requires navigation and the longer arc that provides context for what the navigation is building.

The immediate situation matters. It affects compensation, development, daily experience, and near-term trajectory. These tools exist because the immediate situation cannot be ignored or wished away. But the immediate situation is not the arc. It is a data point on the arc, one that shapes the curve but does not define it.

Careers, viewed at sufficient distance, reveal a pattern that is invisible from within any single role: the compound effect of consistent behavior across time. The professional who operates with integrity, builds credibility, develops others, and navigates organizational complexity with strategic composure does not see the compound effect in any single quarter. They see it across decades: in the reputation that opens doors before they arrive, in the relationships that survive organizational change, in the capability that deepens with each new context, and in the professional identity that becomes, over time, the most durable asset they possess.

The professional who focuses only on the immediate, who optimizes for each situation without reference to the arc, may navigate any single challenge effectively. But they may also discover that a career assembled from reactive decisions lacks the coherence, the compounding, and the legacy that deliberate operation produces.

What Compounds

Viewed individually, these are tools: a framework for diagnosis, a method for emotional regulation, a system for documentation, a model for political navigation. Viewed collectively, they describe a professional operating system that, applied consistently over time, produces compound returns that far exceed the sum of individual applications.

Capability compounds. The diagnostic skill developed in Part I does not remain at its initial level. It deepens with each new situation: each new leader diagnosed, each new organizational dynamic understood. The professional who has navigated three dysfunctional leaders has a diagnostic repertoire that the professional navigating their first cannot match. The translation skill does not remain a single-context tool. It generalizes into a communication capability that serves every professional interaction: upward, lateral, external. Each application refines it. Each refinement makes the next application more effective.

Credibility compounds. The Credibility Compound was introduced as a principle of reputation-building. Across a career, it becomes the professional's most powerful asset. The reputation built over ten years of consistent reliability, visible competence, and professional integrity does not reset when you change roles or organizations. It travels: through references, through the network, through the professional community that remembers your name and what it represents. The early investments in credibility produce returns that accelerate over time, as each new context provides another platform for demonstrating the consistency that the Compound requires.

Relationships compound. The professional who builds genuine, reciprocal relationships across each role (not transactional networking, but the real professional connections that emerge from shared work, mutual respect, and authentic engagement) accumulates a network that becomes exponentially valuable over time. Each new role adds connections. Former colleagues become industry contacts. Former peers become senior leaders in other organizations. The network does not deplete; it grows, and its value grows faster than its size, because the trust embedded in long-standing relationships multiplies the value of each connection.

Leadership identity compounds. The counter-curriculum, the authority-free leadership practice, the self-monitoring discipline: these are not static achievements. They develop. The leader who practices attribution for five years does not attribute the same way they did in year one. The practice has deepened into instinct. The self-monitoring that began as effortful becomes habitual. The leadership identity that started as conscious counter-modeling becomes — over time and through sustained practice — simply who you are.

What the long game produces: a professional whose capabilities, credibility, relationships, and leadership identity have compounded across a career into something no single role created and no single situation can diminish.

Elena's Arc

Elena Vasquez is not at the end of her story. She is closer to the beginning of the arc she has been building toward.

Six months ago she was a frustrated Senior Program Manager under a Conflict Avoider, passed over for promotion twice, losing confidence in the system she operated within. Today she is leading cross-functional initiatives in a new role, under a director who develops his people, on a trajectory toward the management position she once assumed was blocked.

The transformation is real. But Elena sees it with a clarity that she would not have had before navigating David.

"If you'd asked me two years ago what I wanted, I would have said the promotion," Elena reflects. "Get promoted, move up, prove my value. That was the entire frame. What I didn't see was that the promotion isn't the thing. The capability is the thing. The person I had to become to navigate David — the diagnostic thinking, the emotional regulation, the strategic positioning, the political awareness — that's what changed my trajectory. Not the transfer. Not the new director. The capability I built because I had to."

She pauses. "David didn't develop me. Let's be clear about that. He didn't mentor me or invest in my growth or do any of the things a competent leader does. But the situation he created required me to develop myself in ways that a comfortable situation never would have. I built infrastructure that I now use every day — and none of it was part of his plan. It was part of mine."

Elena is looking forward now. The management role is visible. Her director has told her directly that she is being positioned for it. The timeline is months, not years. She will enter that role with a set of capabilities that most first-time managers do not possess: the ability to diagnose team dynamics, the discipline of emotional regulation under pressure, the practice of direct feedback, the infrastructure of distributed credibility, the political fluency to navigate organizational complexity, and the self-monitoring to ensure that the patterns she absorbed do not become the patterns she transmits. The influence-based leadership she practiced without authority (direction through clarity, credibility through competence, investment in development, coordination through relationship) will now carry the weight of a formal role.

"I will be a better manager because of what I navigated," Elena says. "Not because suffering is educational — it isn't, automatically. Because I chose to treat it as education. I studied what was happening. I built tools. I didn't just survive David. I used the experience to become someone who can lead."

Marcus's Horizon

Marcus Chen has been operating strategically for fourteen years. His perspective is longer than Elena's and, in some ways, quieter.

The equity has vested. The golden handcuffs opened three months ago. The calculation Marcus has been running, quarter after quarter, variable after variable, has reached its conclusion. The variable that anchored him to his current situation no longer applies.

Marcus has not left.

"The calculation changed when the equity vested," Marcus confirms. "But not in the direction I expected. I assumed that once the financial constraint lifted, I would move. The external options exist. The market values my experience. But when I ran the full assessment — trajectory, timing, direction, narrative, relationships — staying became the strategic choice. Not because of James. Because of the team."

The forty people Marcus leads have become, over the past three years, something he did not fully anticipate when he was focused on navigating James. They have become a legacy in progress.

"I've watched six people on my team get promoted in three years," Marcus says. "Two of them are now managing their own teams, and they manage well — they attribute, they develop, they make decisions with operational understanding. They lead the way I tried to lead them. That's not something I want to walk away from to optimize my own title."

Marcus's career trajectory has not stalled under James. It has found a dimension that his earlier strategic calculations did not fully account for: the impact on people. The professionals he has developed will carry his influence forward. Not his name, not his credit, but the patterns of leadership he modeled and the capabilities he helped them build. That impact outlasts any position, any title, any compensation package.

"James is still James," Marcus adds. "The dysfunction hasn't changed. But my relationship to it has. I've built the infrastructure to operate effectively despite it. And the team I've built is producing outcomes that even James can't obscure.

The external market will be there when the timing is right. Right now, the timing is right for what I'm building here."

Marcus will move eventually. The Strategic Operator always maintains options, always tracks the variables, always keeps the calculation current. But the choice to stay, made from strength, with full information, in service of a longer objective than personal advancement, reflects the maturity of a professional who has been playing the long game for over a decade.

The Professional Legacy Framework

Legacy is a word usually reserved for the end of a career. The Strategic Operator begins building it much earlier, because legacy is not what you leave behind when you finish. It is what you build while you work.

Five dimensions of professional impact compound across a career and constitute the lasting residue of a professional life.

Capability transferred. The knowledge, skills, and judgment you have developed, and, critically, shared. The professional who accumulates expertise but never transfers it leaves behind a gap when they depart. The professional who develops others — who teaches, mentors, and builds capability around them — leaves behind an asset that continues producing value long after they have moved on. Every professional Elena develops in her future management role carries forward the capability she built. Every team member Marcus has invested in carries forward the operational excellence and leadership discipline he modeled.

Standards established. The norms of behavior, quality, and professionalism you create in the environments you influence. The team that operates with integrity because its leader modeled integrity. The department that attributes specifically because its director insisted on specific attribution. The project that was documented thoroughly because the program manager built documentation into the culture. Standards, once established, persist beyond the individual who created them, particularly when they are embedded in practices rather than enforced through personality.

Relationships sustained. The professional network built across a career, the genuine, reciprocal relationships that survive role changes, organizational departures, and the passage of time. These relationships are not instrumental. They are the connective tissue of a professional life: the colleagues who become lifelong contacts, the mentees who become peers, the leaders who remember you as someone worth recommending. The quality of these relationships reflects the quality of the professional who built them.

Patterns broken. Perhaps the most significant dimension: the dysfunctional patterns you chose not to transmit. Every cycle of dysfunction that ends with you, because you identified it, monitored for it, and corrected it, is a legacy that protects every professional who works under your leadership. The Conflict Avoider's avoidance, stopped. The Credit Absorber's appropriation, reversed. The Micromanager's control, released. Each broken pattern is an inheritance you did not pass on.

The example you set. Not the curated, performative example of organizational role-modeling, but how you operated under pressure, how you treated people when no one with authority was watching, and how you navigated complexity without abandoning your values. The professionals who work with you observe everything. The example you set — in composure, in integrity, in how you handle dysfunction without becoming it — is the most durable curriculum you offer.

The Strategic Operator: Full Synthesis

The Introduction posed five diagnostic questions. The answers have changed.

Diagnostic clarity. The pattern has a name. The system that produced it is visible. Frustration has been replaced by structural understanding.

Emotional stability. Composure operates as infrastructure, not effort. The reactive professional who began this journey has built the regulation that makes strategic action possible.

Upward influence. Translation is practiced. Communication adapts to the receiver. Documentation creates evidence that exists independent of anyone's memory or advocacy.

Career positioning. The political landscape is mapped. Visibility is engineered. Movement is a calculation, not a crisis.

Leadership development. The counter-curriculum is active. Authority-free leadership is in practice. The patterns observed are being inverted, not absorbed.

The distance between those two sets of answers is what the system produces.

DIAGNOSE. STABILIZE. INFLUENCE. POSITION. EVOLVE. The five phases cycle through every new role, every new leader, every new organizational context. Each iteration is faster and deeper. The Strategic Operator who has internalized them does not consult a checklist. They operate from an orientation: strategic without being calculating, composed without detachment, aware without cynicism.

What Actually Matters

At the end of a career, what remains?

Not the titles, which expire when you leave. Not the quarterly results that felt so urgent at the time.

What remains is simpler and harder to measure.

The people you developed: professionals who are better at what they do because you invested in them, gave them feedback, and modeled the behaviors they now carry forward. The patterns you broke and the standard you held: the consistency of doing the right thing reliably, treating people well under pressure, and operating with integrity when it was not required.

The professional who can look back at a career and see these things has built something that organizational dysfunction cannot easily diminish and no single leadership failure can define. They played the long game. And what they built compounds — not into victory, but into a professional life that justifies the discipline it required.

This book began with a premise: leadership quality is an environmental variable, but career trajectory is not. The organizations you work in will not reliably provide competent leadership. The systems designed to identify, develop, and retain effective leaders will continue to fail in predictable ways. The professional who waits for the system to work as advertised will wait a long time.

The Strategic Operator does not wait. They diagnose, stabilize, influence, position, and evolve. They treat their career as something they engineer — deliberately, strategically, with the long view that transforms a sequence of jobs into a professional arc.

Elena Vasquez will become a manager. She will lead with the capability that adversity developed, the counter-curriculum that observation provided, and the self-awareness that navigating dysfunction built. Her team will operate under the conditions David could not provide — because she will build them deliberately.

Marcus Chen will continue to build. Whether he stays or moves, he will decide strategically. His impact will outlast his current position. The forty people he leads are already carrying forward the leadership patterns he modeled. His legacy is the standard he set and the people he developed.

The dysfunction will not end. The organizations will not fix themselves.

But you have built the infrastructure to operate within them. That is what the system produces.

Selected Reading

The following works informed the broader intellectual landscape surrounding organizational behavior, power dynamics, leadership development, and professional sustainability. They are not prerequisites for this book. They represent adjacent thinking for readers who wish to deepen their understanding of the systems within which they operate.

Laurence J. Peter — The Peter Principle
A foundational articulation of structural promotion failure — the tendency for organizations to elevate individuals beyond their competence.

Jeffrey Pfeffer — Power: Why Some People Have It — and Others Don't
A rigorous examination of how power operates inside organizations, and why political skill is often decisive in career trajectory.

Chris Argyris — Overcoming Organizational Defenses
A study of defensive routines within institutions and the ways organizations unintentionally preserve dysfunction.

Christina Maslach & Michael Leiter — The Burnout Challenge
Research-backed exploration of burnout dynamics, particularly the role of ambiguity, misalignment, and effort-reward imbalance.

Herminia Ibarra — Act Like a Leader, Think Like a Leader
An exploration of leadership identity development, especially the evolution from individual contributor to influence-based leadership.

Ronald Heifetz & Marty Linsky — Leadership on the Line
A systems-oriented perspective on authority, adaptive leadership, and the risks inherent in challenging organizational norms.

Daniel Kahneman — Thinking, Fast and Slow
A foundational examination of cognitive bias and decision-making distortions that influence judgment at every organizational level.

www.ingramcontent.com/pod-product-compliance
Lightning Source LLC
LaVergne TN
LVHW010703110826
845149LV00014B/3217

* 9 7 8 1 9 7 2 1 9 4 0 4 1 *